MW01707461

This book is dedicated to...

...each and everyone who wants to
create the best life possible.

Table of contents

Introduction

By the time I was seven I had my own office. It was located in a tree house high above the ground, way up, from the rest of the world. Back then, much of my deep thinking was done in this tree house. I often spent long moments pondering about the future and how things would turn out when I became older. It was in this tree house this book really began. In those thoughts the seed of my lifelong dream began to grow. A dream of helping people: Helping people by teaching them how to really feel good and inspire them to make positive changes in their life.

Have you ever considered how it all works – feeling good that is? How do you create good and pleasant feelings? If there is anything we can be sure of, it is that you are doing something. Just the same as there are recipes for your success, there are also recipes for your feelings. I have devoted my whole life since my tree house days to studying this recipe. A recipe I call the positive aspects of life.

Research shows that optimists are healthier and live significantly longer than pessimists. Looking at health and longevity, it is at least as dangerous to be pessimistic as it is to be a smoker. The average person has about 40,000 thoughts each day and studies have pointed to the fact that almost 90% of these thoughts are negative. This is a scary prospect considering that negative thoughts damage our brains. As the old saying goes: "What goes in must come out" and the brain works just the same way.

Throughout life, we search for thousands of answers. Sometimes we travel great distances in search of these answers, but the most important answers are most often found if we turn our gaze inwards, into our own hearts. This book is meant to be read by everyone ready to make some small changes in their lives in order to feel even better. I want to give you effective tools, methods and tips that will make your life easier and lead to a better and happier life.

1
One year left to live

Right before we take our last breath something happens. Valuable insights, previously unknown and unnoticed, all of a sudden become clearer than ever before.

Would you keep living the way you do today if you only had one year left to live? Would you value the same things, think along the same lines or would you change your life?

When we lie on our deathbed and think back on our lives, almost everyone tends to regret a number of things. When we are right in the middle of things, busy living out our lives, it is hard to hit the pause button and give ourselves time to reflect. When someone's life is about to end, however, new insights usually manifest themselves. We see things from a different angle, from a different perspective. Maybe this is because we slow down, or maybe it is because we finally have the courage to be honest with ourselves.

A few years ago, an Australian nurse by the name of Bronnie Ware wrote a book about what people tend to regret when their lives are drawing to a close. She was tending to patients who were close to dying and claims that there are primarily five things people tend to regret:

1. *I wish I'd had the courage to live a life true to myself, not the life others expected of me.*
"This was the most common regret of all. When people realise that their life is almost over and look back clearly on it, it is easy to see how many dreams have gone unfulfilled. Most people had not honored even a half of their dreams and had to die knowing that it was due to choices they had made, or not made. Health brings a freedom very few realise, until they no longer have it."

2. *I wish I didn't work so hard.*
"This came from every male patient that I nursed. They missed their children's youth and their partner's companionship. All of the men I nursed deeply regretted spending so much of their lives on the treadmill of a work existence."

3. *I wish I'd had the courage to express my feelings.*
"Many people suppressed their feelings in order to keep peace with others. As a result, they settled for a mediocre existence and never became who they were truly capable of becoming. Many developed illnesses relating to the bitterness and resentment they carried as a result."

4. *I wish I had stayed in touch with my friends.*
"Often they would not truly realise the full benefits of old friends until their dying weeks and it was not always possible to track them down. Many had become so caught up in their own lives that they had let golden friendships slip by over the years. There were many deep regrets about not giving friendships the time and effort that they deserved. Everyone misses their friends when they are dying."

5. *I wish that I had let myself be happier.*
"This is a surprisingly common one. Many did not realise until the end that happiness is a choice. They had stayed stuck in old patterns and habits. The so-called 'comfort' of familiarity overflowed into their emotions, as well as their physical lives. Fear of change had them pretending to others, and to their selves, that they were content. When deep within, they longed to laugh properly and have silliness in their life again."

You do not find long-term happiness by having the perfect life or by meeting your dream partner. Long-term happiness is found within yourself through your actions here and now, in your everyday life.

If you are looking to buy a new home, you probably have a clear picture how you want it to look to enjoy living there. The same probably goes when buying a new car – you most likely have an idea of what kind of car would best fulfill your needs. In the workplace, there are always instructions for the employees. These instructions aim to clarify the tasks of the employee and the goal is to make sure that both employer and employee get the most out of the exchange. The question now is how you make sure that you get the most out of your life. How do you make sure that you are living the life you actually could be living? Maybe it's impossible to avoid having regrets on your deathbed, but wouldn't it be foolish to not even try?

Most people have a pretty good idea of what they want out of life. Putting these thoughts down on paper, however, they become clearer, more concrete and comprehensible. What I propose is that you take a moment to sit down, grab a pen and paper and write something that could be called "Guidelines for my life."

Here, you simply put down what you need in your life in order to live it to the fullest. Write down what you want your life to look like when it comes to family, interests, work, leisure, friends and so on. Describe what really matters to you and what gives you meaning.

Imagine that you had only one year left to live and put down what you would like to accomplish during this time and what you would like to experience. How would you like to spend your free time? Who would you like to spend time with and how would you like to interact with your family, partner, friends, colleagues and everyone around you? Look inwards and consider what your ideal life could look like.

If you are in a relationship, I suggest that you and your partner each write your own life guidelines. When you are both done, the two of you tell each other what you wrote and discuss how you would like your relationship to evolve. Think about how you would prefer to spend your time together. Maybe you both love Broadway musicals or going to the movies together, then decide how often you would like to do these things. Also, put down how often you want to have family dinners, meet other couples, travel, take walks together, just having nights staying in and so on.

Perhaps you estimate that you have ten, or maybe even fifty, years left to live. What if you are cheated? Cheated out of your life? What if you only have one year left?

Imagine for a minute that you are told that you only have one year left to live, and that you have also reached the point where you have accepted this situation. Imagine that you are taking a stroll along the beach. Would you kick off your shoes to enjoy the feeling of sand between your toes, enjoying the birds singing and listening to children laughing and playing? Would you experience nature's wonderful scents, look in wonder at the shifting colors of the sky above, watch the ocean and marvel at its vastness? Would you experience happiness and joy seeing an old couple walking towards you and then, all of a sudden, stopping to hug each other?

If you only had one year left to live, would you embrace life differently and would you enjoy all of life's sensory inputs differently than you do today?

2
Feel good every day

Some people just seem very fortunate. They are always happy and positive. How come they're so lucky? These positive people must have bad days too, or are they simply so positive because they never run into problems? Of course not. In my view, these people, who we see as perpetually positive, have something in common.

I can guarantee you that happy and positive people have just as many problems as the rest of us. The difference is that they focus on the things that create pleasant feelings. But how do we do this? How do we focus on those things that make us feel good when there are so many distracting thoughts and feelings in the way? Let us look at some methods that may be very helpful to you.

Reinforce your positive feelings

It is all too easy to focus on the bad aspects of life. Often, we tend to focus on what is missing instead of really noticing what we already have in our lives: "What if I had a better place to live, if I were thinner, if I had a life partner, if I were single, if I had more money, if my job was more interesting, if I – for just this one time – could just have some luck."

When we think about what we miss or the bad aspects of life, we remind ourselves of those very things that are bad or the things we miss. What we really need to do is just the opposite. We need to remind ourselves of what we like about our lives and to focus on what we actually have. If we do this, we reinforce what we appreciate. This, in turn, makes us feel much better.

Imagine a Monday morning having coffee with your colleagues. One of your colleagues asks you: "So, what's up?" You reply that: "You know…Monday. Another week of hustle and bustle ahead of us. It's no picnic." Here, in this example, you reinforce your feeling of what is tough, and you do this by reminding yourself of what you find so hard about Mondays. Since you want to feel as good as possible, another possible reply could be along the lines of: "Well, it's Monday. I had a great weekend with my family and I feel pretty well-rested. Besides, I have an interesting meeting at ten o'clock, so I have a lot going for me right now." Here, on the contrary, you remind yourself of what is good and this reinforces your positive feelings.

Some of the most common triggers for negative thoughts are just Mondays, rain, stress, rude people and being tired. These triggers are always waiting to pounce on you. They are very strong and they can hit you when you least expect it. But these negativity triggers can be outsmarted. The way I see it, this is exactly what genuinely positive people have in common. They outfox life's negativity triggers by instead choosing to focus on what they appreciate. These people are good at accepting situations that cannot be altered – like Mondays or bad weather. They know that it is impossible to change the weather, and instead they choose to accept the bad storm and make sure that it is extra cozy inside. This, in turn, makes them feel better. These people focus on finding solutions to their problems and finding opportunities when things are rough.

Positive people have often taught themselves to focus on what makes them feel good, instead of focusing on what makes them feel bad. Furthermore, studies have also shown that happy people have a perspective on life and a behavior that constantly rewards them with positive experiences.

Put your problems in perspective

A few years ago, on a rainy day, I pulled over on the highway to help an elderly man whose car had broken down. Normally, it is pretty aggravating when your car breaks down in the middle of the highway but strangely enough, this man seemed completely unaffected. He was looking at his car with an almost philosophical twinkle in his eyes, and while the rain was pouring down on him, he was even smiling. The fact that he was soaking wet and that his car would not start did not seem to face him in the least.

Obviously, I was very keen to find out what was going on in his mind. So I asked him. His reply was that at first he was annoyed, but then he started to think about all the good things he had in life. He felt that he had so much in life he treasured, and all of this sort of overtook him to the degree that there was no room for minor car problems. Most people would have focused on the problem at hand (i.e. the broken-down car), and subsequently reinforced the negative feeling stemming from this annoying situation.

It is very natural to be annoyed when stuck in a difficult situation. But at these times, take the opportunity to remind yourself of what makes you happy. Then you put your problems in perspective and often the perceived problem fades. Just because you have a headache, your knee hurts or you are stressed about work does not mean that your whole life is bad. All the things you treasure are still there.

Find nuances in your negative thoughts

Try to view different situations and experiences in different nuances. When you do this, you present your brain with different perspectives. Let us say that it is freezing cold outside. You can then choose to view this cold in two different shades. One says that it is icy and bone-chillingly cold outside, while the other one says that the weather is beautiful and crisp. If you come across problems at work, you can decide to focus on a difficult task or decide to focus on what you will have learned when you solve the problem. Even a situation that at first glance feels like pure tragedy may instead be a great possibility. If, for instance, you are made redundant at your job, then this could lead to you having the opportunity to fulfill your dream of starting your own business. Being fired could also lead you to a better job.

We always have a choice. We can almost always choose to look at a situation, event or experience in different shades.

Create an expectation

Creating an enhanced effect through anticipation could be compared to the placebo effect, which takes place when our pain recedes after taking a sugar pill. This happens because we believe the pill will reduce our pain. When we are given a pill we believe will reduce pain, our body initiates its own morphine system. This is the same system that is initiated when we are given real, pain-reducing, morphine.

In 2002, The New England Journal of Medicine published a study on a group of people with serious pain in their knees. These patients were divided into three groups, where two groups underwent two different standard procedures. For the third group, however, the procedure was bogus. The patients were anesthetized, a few cuts were made around their knees, which were then stitched together. The surgeon then talked to the patients as if the procedures had really taken place. The results of this study were astounding. The pain for the patients in the "placebo group" was reduced to the same extent as for the patients who had undergone actual procedures.

When you are travelling, you expect to be able to enjoy life and to experience new things. A sense of curiosity is awakened, which makes you open your eyes towards life. You are interested in cathedrals, museums and interesting places. You appreciate your new experiences and impressions, and you appreciate every single day of your vacation abroad. Back home, in your everyday life, it is harder to feel the same level of satisfaction. Your interest in cathedrals and beautiful buildings is not nearly as big. This is because we do not have the same expectation of seeing life as pleasurable when we are back home. Our expectations to experience beautiful buildings are also lower. A consequence of this is that we often do not even notice beautiful buildings in our surroundings. But things do not have to be this way. Just because we are back in our everyday lives does not mean that we cannot be just as content with life as when we are on holiday.

In order to create the same power in our experience and pleasure, we need to create an expectation. We need to create an expectation about tomorrow or the weekend, just as we do when we are on vacation. I promise you that there are loads of beautiful and interesting things to see and experience in your surroundings, things you have not yet discovered.

In your everyday life, there is much more of a risk that some days feel heavy, but I know that even these days have their bright spots. Imagine if you were able to see these bright spots even when you are experiencing darkness. I know that we can learn to live a more positive life and that we can learn how to guide our thoughts to create a feeling of satisfaction. I also know that we can learn to feel good pretty much every day of our lives.

Do you remember how you used to feel as a kid the day before Christmas? Most likely, you had a certain expectation about the following day. Before you fell asleep, you were thinking about Santa Claus, presents and maybe Christmas candy. One could say that you had a dream the day before Christmas about this magnificent day. Do you remember what it felt like as a kid when you woke up on Christmas? My guess is that you did not have any problems getting out of bed. I am sure that you were in a terrific mood, full of expectations and positive thoughts and feelings.

Wouldn't it be nice if we fell asleep every night with the premonition that tomorrow will be a dream day, just like the dream about Christmas? Imagine if we could create this feeling before we fall asleep each night. Imagine going to sleep with a feeling that tomorrow will be like a dream. As kids, we were able to create this feeling and this is still possible for us as adults. The minutes before you fall asleep determine what kind of mood you will be in when you wake up the next day. We have all heard stories about people trying to solve problems before going to sleep. They fail, but when they wake up the day after, they can clearly see a solution to their problems. Relationship experts say that we should go to sleep as friends. I would like to emphasize that we should go to sleep with happy feelings every night. The thoughts and feelings you fall asleep to will grow stronger as you sleep.

One way to recreate the feeling we could call "The dream about Christmas" is that you light a candle right before you go to sleep. Lie down comfortably and think about the things you appreciate in life. Think about what makes you happy. Think about someone you care for or something you look forward to. Maybe you plan to take a nice walk in the woods tomorrow or maybe have a cup of coffee with a good friend. Why not think about something fun or relaxing you plan to do during the weekend? Ban troubling or difficult thoughts and devote this moment completely to the things that make you feel warm inside. After a moment or two, you will have a pleasant feeling in your body as you blow out the candle and hopefully go to sleep feeling completely content.

The day after, when the alarm goes off, you probably still have this nice feeling and you will be able to start your new day feeling completely at ease. Maybe you will even be able to start the day with a certain amount of expectation and eagerness regarding all the challenges and good things the day has to offer. All days have good things to offer. Some days these are just harder to notice, but not today.

The Golden hour

As we get out of bed in the morning, the hour I believe to be the most important hour of the day begins. Let us call this "The golden hour." This hour will set the tone for the rest of the day. If you start your day by oversleeping, wolf down a sandwich or two before you rush off to work, there is a pretty good risk that this hurried and stressed feeling will stick with you during a big chunk of the day. This feeling could make you irritable and could also lead to a number of distractions throughout the day. We have to treat our mornings with care. Maybe it is a good idea to get up a bit earlier. Or why not treat yourself to a really good breakfast? Perhaps you can squeeze in some alone time to read a newspaper and have a nice cup of coffee, or maybe get some quality time with your family.

It is all about creating habits and routines that will make you feel good in the long run. At first, it is often difficult to change familiar routines and thought patterns, but if you do this often enough, these changes will become a natural part of your life.

Make a fist

When we smile, we feel happier. When we stand tall, we feel stronger. And when we make a fist, we send out a signal to our inner self that something is good. In the world of sports, it is very common to give yourself encouraging signals like, for instance, making a fist. Your body has a direct effect on your well-being. Consider how you can use your body to feel as good as possible. We are all triggered by different things. For some, making a fist is the best, whereas others stretch out and take a few deep breaths. Some simply raise their arms towards the sky and smile.

Don't take yourself too seriously

What does it really matter if we make fools out of ourselves, say the wrong things or make a mistake? Life could end tomorrow or we could live to be a hundred years old. Regardless, we are not bad people just because we make fools out of ourselves or make mistakes. No one is more important than anyone else and making mistakes is a part of life. Practice putting yourself in perspective and try to be as generous as possible towards the people around you that a mistake here and there is no skin off your back. Have you noticed that most things eventually tend to work themselves out in the end?

Focus on the "reward"

Instead of focusing on the negative feeling that it is Monday, focus on how good it will feel when your workday is over. You may visualize how you enjoy a good meal after work. Instead of dwelling on how difficult it will be to have that delicate conversation with your friend, think about how good it will feel afterwards. If we learn how to focus on the right things, life becomes much easier – not only for ourselves, but also for those around us.

Don't pay attention to your mental figments

I know that life sometimes feels difficult. You have not had enough sleep, you have no inspiration, no energy, the boss is a pain in the neck and no one seems to understand you. Is it really possible to turn a day like that around? Is there anything you can do to feel good for at least part of the day, or even the whole day? I would argue that you can turn all bad days into at least relatively good ones.

If, for instance, you are at work and your feelings of hopelessness and total fatigue seem insurmountable, then stop thinking about all the things leading to these difficult feelings. When you are very tired or when you feel overwhelmed by difficulties, it is often a matter of mental figments. If you say to them: "Welcome, but I don't care about you," then they will soon drift away like clouds in the sky. They simply lose patience.

If, however, you start to analyze them, you give them nourishment and they will stick to your brain even more. Welcome them and they will dissolve themselves. Later, when you are at home and not as tired, you will understand that these thoughts were only the result of you being tired or stressed.

Make an appointment with yourself to work out problems

Sometimes we are feeling bad because we actually have real problems. My suggestion in these cases is that you make an appointment with yourself to work out these problems. When you are at work, you need to focus on the tasks at hand. There is really no room for solving your personal problems while you are working. Most of the time, these difficult feelings just swirl around in your head without you being able to come up with a solution that makes you feel any better. So just say stop and give yourself a break. Decide to go and have a cup of coffee alone after work. This is where you give yourself the quality time you need to face these feelings.

If these thoughts happen to come up at work, say to yourself: "Stop! At five o'clock, when I'm in the coffee shop, I will deal with this. Now, I have to work." What you are really doing here is that you are putting your feelings in a holding pattern in order to return to them later.

Later, when you have the time to consider what creates these negative feelings, it is easier to clarify them by putting them down on paper. You can, in your own time, find solutions for how you are to deal with your boss or whatever kind of problems you are facing. You now have the time to figure out why she is giving you such a hard time. Perhaps there is something you can do to find a better way to deal with her?

In many cases, it turns out that you actually just need this moment to think and reflect, which, in turn, could give you another perspective on the feelings you are experiencing.

Practice accepting your past

In order to evolve and get control over unwanted feelings, it is important to deal with our past. This, however, does not mean that we should dwell on our past too much. When we accept times past as just that, and instead start to look forward, something happens in our lives. We get a feeling of freedom and look towards the future with a higher degree of anticipation.

Take notice of the good times

Someone who only notices when he is feeling bad will develop a sense of always feeling bad, even when this is not the case. The same thing is true at work. If we only notice when our job is really boring, we will eventually start to believe that our job is always boring. If we only notice the cold and rainy days, we will eventually start to feel as if it is always cold and rainy. If there is someone we dislike, it is very easy to only notice that person's bad sides. We simply do not notice when this person shows any positive sides.

Try to notice the positive moments in your day-to-day life and notice the positive sides of those around you. Much will be gained if you succeed in this. First, you will have a better time at your job and your life will be seen in a more positive light – something that will make you feel even better. Second, you will become stronger and more prepared to deal with the difficulties of life as they arise. Third, you will become better at dealing objectively with the shortcomings of those around you if and when these manifest themselves.

Appreciate what is taken for granted

A few years ago, I walked past an old man selling a magazine for the homeless. I got curious as he looked so genuinely happy. He had everything he owned in a shopping cart. His clothes were all worn out and his hands looked as if they were covered in mud. But he seemed happy – happier than most people walking down the sidewalk.

Even though it may not have been completely appropriate, I had to ask him if I could buy him a cup of coffee and something to eat. He gave me a hesitant look but nevertheless accepted my invitation. When he had finished his sandwich, I told him that it made me so happy to see happiness just radiating from him. He looked at me and said: "Well, you see, I slept so well last night. Most of the time, I sleep out on the streets, but last night I was able to sleep in a restroom in a shopping mall. I even managed to gather up a lot of newspapers, so last night I was both warm and comfortable. This morning, I treated myself to a hamburger, so I haven't been all that hungry today. So you're darn right I'm happy!"

This captivating man had learned to appreciate some of the things most people today take for granted. Things like a nice walk, birds singing, fresh air, a smile, being healthy, having a full belly, having a good night's sleep and a roof over your head. Of course, it may be fun buying a new TV or new clothes. This gives us a nice feeling at the time. Maybe it creates some sort of happiness at that particular moment, but it does not create any kind of long-term happiness.

Hans Christian Andersen, the Danish author best known for his fairytales, once said that: "The whole world is a series of miracles, but we're so used to them we call them ordinary things." If we once more would learn to appreciate life's so-called certainties, I am certain that genuine happiness will find us.

Be grateful

Often look back at your happy moments. Look forward to the things that make you happy and try to treasure every ounce of happiness. Try to be grateful – both to yourself and to those around you.

The power of struggling

I can still remember when I was a kid and I used to run around looking for empty soda cans. When I came home, I put the money I had earned in one of my mom's old glass jars. I used to look at the coins and start to dream about the awesome bike I planned to buy some day.

Three months later, the jar was full of coins. I grabbed it and ran down to the best bicycle store in town. Once there, I walked up to the salesman with firm and eager steps. I looked him in the eyes and proudly declared: "I want to buy that bike." That same night, I fell asleep happy as a clam. Next to my bed was my brand new, beautiful bike.

3
Fill your life with meaning

When you fill your life with meaning, you fill your senses with inspiration. This creates wonders in your life.

Your purpose is the foundation of everything you do. All activities need a purpose in order to be useful in the long run. When you work out, your purpose is to feel good. If you start your own business, maybe your purpose is financial in nature or maybe making a dream come true. If you are having dinner with a friend, the purpose is to have a good time. If you are lending support to a friend feeling bad, the purpose is to make your friend feel better. We have a purpose in everything we do, whether it is conscious or subconscious. When we make tough decisions, we may devote a great deal of time thinking about our purpose. Even more important, though, is to consider whether or not you have the right purpose in life. In other words – what is the meaning of your life?

Maybe you think that the meaning of life is to find a partner and have children, or maybe you believe that the meaning of life is simply to have fun.

Someone once said: "The meaning of life is a life with meaning." The fact of the matter is that we can give our lives meaning on a number of different levels. While thinking that the great meaning of life is having children, it is also possible to believe that another meaning of life is to fulfill yourself. Yet another meaning could be to simply enjoy life. In order to develop, while at the same time finding the different levels of meaning, it is necessary that we regularly challenge ourselves.

Greek philosopher Socrates had a rather unique quality. He was very keen to pose questions to those around him and one of his most frequent questions was "why?" This made people more inclined to think.

Today, more than two millennia later, we are well aware of the fact that questioning leads to progress. When you ask yourself questions, you force yourself to think.

This in turn leads to a richer life. I am certain that each and every one of us would benefit from having a small Socrates standing on our shoulder, frequently questioning things and making us stop and reflect.

When we were kids, we asked a lot of questions, but as we grew up something happened – we started to ask less and less questions. This is perhaps just the way things are, but life is really too short to get to know ourselves at a really deep level. Throughout our journey through life, there is also always the risk that we lose ourselves along the way. The curveballs of life can make us evolve in ways that are far from who we really are. If we want to stay as true to ourselves as possible – while continuing to discover new dimensions of ourselves throughout life – we need to stop frequently and ask questions. We are always busy and life is rushing along like a steam train, but the best investment you can possibly make is to press that pause button of yours and give yourself time to reflect. There are a million questions we

could ask ourselves, but I recommend that you steer these questions to areas especially important to you and your future. Like, for example:

The Meaning of life – What gives me a sense of meaning?
Well-being – How do I really feel? What do I need to do in my life to feel as good as possible?
Self-realization – Do I live the life I want to live? Am I at the right place in life? Do I feel at home in my present environment?
Happiness – What is real happiness to me?
Old habits – Are there things in my life I am doing just out of habit?
Personal development – Does it feel as if I am growing? Have I postponed something that is actually very important? Am I reaching my true potential? What are my talents? How can I best benefit from them? What would I like to learn or improve?
Self-awareness – Are there situations where I become overly sensitive or upset, and why? Why do I get nervous in certain situations? Why do I tend to follow the herd? Why don't I realize my dreams? Why do I work at a place I really do not care for? How do I actually treat the people around me?
Self-worth – Am I giving myself the absolute best in life? If not, why? Do I get the respect I deserve from the people around me?
Priorities in life – What gives me energy? Do I like my life?

For obvious reasons, there are situations in life when we cease to think, when we go on autopilot. Unfortunately, a lot of people leave their autopilots on for the whole day. In the morning, they get up and, in a robot-like fashion, talk with their wife, take their children to daycare, work, cook, clean and watch TV before finally going to bed. Sometimes, this robot-like behavior is pure survival instinct.

When we start a new job, it comes naturally for us to ask a lot of questions – both to our new colleagues as well as to ourselves. In the beginning, we learn new things and find the best ways to manage our new job. The longer we stay there, the less we need to think and gradually it becomes more and more routine. Finally, there is the risk that the autopilot takes over.

The big question is whether this is a good thing for our personal growth and whether or not this is a signal that we really should get a new job, or at least new tasks. Even more troubling, however, is that some people let their autopilot remain on throughout their everyday lives, among friends and family. Like a robot, they practice their hobbies and spend time with their children and life partner.

Some aspects in life are pure routine. We do certain things because we have always done so, and therefore it is a good idea to sometimes stop and ask "why?" For example: "Why do I still work at a job I don't like? Why do I still play golf once a week, even though I don't like it anymore?"

Another interesting question you may ask yourself is: "What does this mean?" Let us say that you are offered a new job and that you persist on asking yourself this one question:

If I take this job, what does this mean?
Higher salary.

If I get a higher salary, what does this mean to me and my life?
More freedom.

If I get more freedom in my life, what does this mean?
I can travel and enjoy life more.

If I can travel and enjoy life more, what does this mean?
I will be happier.

If I become happier, what does this mean?
I will become a better person and life will be easier.

What does this mean?
If I am happy and a better person, it benefits both me as well as those around me.

Initially, it may seem that the purpose of getting a new job was to make more money, but, looking at it more carefully, it turned out that your real purpose was different. What really turned out to be meaningful to you was simply that you and those around you are feeling good.

Aaron Antonowski, professor in medical sociology, studied why certain individuals are able to cope with tough challenges, while others suffer from stress. He studied a group of women who had been concentration camp inmates. Despite deeply traumatic experiences, some of these women were relatively stable and were able to live functioning lives later on. Antonowski's aim was to find out what was different about these women compared to those who had not been able to go on and live good, functioning lives after being liberated from the concentration camp.

He came to the conclusion that the women who managed to recreate their lives and feel relatively well after this trauma looked upon their current existence as comprehensible, manageable and meaningful. Antonowski went on to coin the term "Sense of Coherence" (SOC).

Comprehensibility means that I have a sense of understanding the world around me, as well as my own feelings, and that I look upon existence as predictable.

In other words, I have a sense of understanding what is happening in my life. I understand, for example, why I have the job I have and why my life looks the way it does.

Manageability is about having the sense of possessing the tools necessary to meet all of life's demands. Putting it simply, I feel that I can manage my life. For example, I have a sense of being able to manage my job and the rest of my life.

Meaningfulness means that I have a sense of participating in the world. I am willing to invest my commitment and energy into life's challenges. I feel, for instance, that my role in the workplace is important and that my life has meaning.

According to Antonowski and his research, these three factors are crucial for how we deal with the hardships and challenges of life. Everyone obviously wants to have meaning in their lives, but how do we improve our sense of meaningfulness? Sometimes it is possible that we feel that our lives have meaning through someone else, but the feeling is always grounded within ourselves. What is meaningful goes back to what we have experienced in life and differs vastly from individual to individual.

The sense of meaning is created in our own minds and may be recognized through our own experiences and feelings. There are many indications that the key to long-term happiness is filling your life with meaning. When you feel that your life is meaningful, you have a purpose in life.

Perhaps you already have a great sense of meaning in everything you do, or perhaps you have a deep longing for meaning. Regardless, I hope that the following may inspire you to create more meaning in your life.

Love

The love of our children, life partner and even animals is probably the number one source of meaning.

Value yourself

As you start to value yourself, you start to raise your expectations about life. This will, consciously as well as subconsciously, lead you to having an increased sense of meaning in your life.

Be yourself

As we step out of our everyday roles and instead let us be led by our inner voice, we become more true to ourselves. This helps us to live in the here and now. When we are true to ourselves, it is easier to live our own lives and not someone else's. It is easier for us to resist the expectations from those around us about how we should live our lives.

Make your dreams come true

Having dreams creates a sense of meaning, but being on track towards realizing one is incredibly powerful.

Influence every important situation

When you influence someone or something in a certain direction, you will experience a sense of meaning.

See your own valuable part in what you do

Try to see the value of what you do in all situations. Regardless of whether you play a large or a small part at work, your share is a part of a bigger picture and it is always important.

Understand why you are doing the things you do

The more aware you are of why you are doing something, the greater the sense of meaning you will experience. Before a workout, for instance, you may remind yourself that the reason for going to the gym is actually to feel better.

Do what you believe in

Going to a job and performing a task you do not believe in is not the way to creating a sense of meaning. If, on the other hand, you do something you know is important in one way or another, then you are more likely to have meaning in your life.

Have fun

When you have fun, you experience joy. And, when you share your fun with someone else, chances are that you will have even more fun. Your time here on Earth is limited, so make sure that you have fun – a lot of fun.

Be present

Your level of being present is directly correlated to your sense of meaning (see chapter 25).

Be grateful

Instead of focusing on what you wish for, it is better to focus on what you already have. Your ability to be grateful influences your sense of meaning. Remember that the great moments of life often take place in life's small moments.

When I was six years old, I remember my grandparents sitting next to one another in their separate rocking chairs. They had lived together their whole lives and were both in their mid-80s. This particular night, they were sitting watching TV and holding hands. All of a sudden, my grandfather takes a deep look into my grandmother's warm eyes and says: "Ah, life is good!" My grandfather was a very wise and fascinating man, with the ability to always feel and express his gratefulness in all kinds of situations. It made no difference whether we were out walking, having a nice meal together or visiting a museum. He always said: "Ah, life is good!"

Use your talents as much as you can

Everyone has talents. Consider whether you have some hidden talent. It is certainly a sad fact that some people live their whole lives without being aware of their talents. Consider how you can use your talents as much as possible.

Spend a lot of time on what you like

Be careful and prioritize what and to whom you give your time to. Aim to do the things you love and try to avoid the things you do not enjoy.

Evaluate your friends

Almost every one of us has a friend we only keep in touch with because of old habits. Everyone changes and sometimes you evolve in different directions. Sometimes both parties may benefit from simply going their separate ways. This does not mean that you do not like this person. It could just be the case that you have grown apart. Just like people grow apart in relationships, people can grow apart as friends.

Your circle of friends affects you more than you think. American author and motivational speaker Jim Rohn once said: "You are the average of the five people you spend the most time with." I think this is a good way to emphasize the need to evaluate and to create a circle of friends that gives you what you want.

Do not be afraid to let go of relationships that give you nothing. This could be people who do nothing but drain you of energy, people who are too judgmental or people who do not respect you. Or it could be people who are dishonest, people who do not share your joy and success or people who do not let you grow.

Create a sense of belonging

Usually, you create a sense of belonging through your family, co-workers and friends, or through some kind of hobby where you meet likeminded people.

Give support to others

By helping others, you contribute to a bigger context, which often gives a sense of meaning. Make other people happy.

Listen

When you listen to somebody, you get a glimpse into another person's life. What is this person really saying and what is being said between the lines? That you really listen and understand is very important to the people around you. This, in turn, gives you a higher sense of meaning.

Create room for the passions in your life

The greater the joy you feel, the greater the sense of meaning you experience. Today, about a third of our time is taken up by our job. Consider if there is anything you can do to be able to work with your passion. The stronger you feel about something, the more you will achieve. Keep in mind that it is possible to transform your big passion into becoming your job.

It has been said that the healthiest and happiest people are those who devote themselves to their passions every day. Furthermore, it turns out that passions that benefit others have an even greater impact on perceived happiness.

Almost everyone has undiscovered passions. A lot of people live their whole lives without discovering their strongest passions. Instead, they focus on worldly success. But what if success finds you as you are enjoying your great passion? Never stop exploring what lights up that spark inside of you.

"Give the world the best you have."

Mother Teresa

4
Your personal truths

Regardless of whether or not you are living the life you want to live, your life is filled with a certain content. You consist of a great number of values, opinions, thoughts and feelings. Some things you love, whereas others scare you. The question now is whether the life you have built comes from within yourself or whether it is the result of the expectations of the people around you. What if you are actually living someone else's life?

We are born with a number of basic emotions and instincts, but, for the most part, it is possible to say that we start out life as a blank sheet of paper. In many ways, we are completely pristine, but with each passing day we pick things up. Everything happening around us is observed and processed, and we learn a great deal every day. In the beginning of our lives, almost everything is passed down to us from our parents. Whether we want to or not, what we experience as children will affect us much more than we think. If you hear something often enough, it eventually becomes a truth to you. That does not mean, however, that this is actually true. To illustrate this, let us compare two invented, but typical, families.

In family number one, the parents are very free-spirited. They are confident and believe that everything is possible. In their world, there are no limits. They prioritize their dreams and have strong faith that they can be realized. They are also aware of the strong influence they have, and will continue to have, on the future of their children. Because of this, they are constantly encouraging their children in everything they do. Their children are told every day that: "You can do it. You're amazing! Everything is possible for you. You can become anything you like. We believe in you." When one of the daughters fails trying to do something, the parents say: "Great that you took the initiative and tried. The next time you'll succeed, because now you know how to do it." These children create a truth for themselves that everything is possible. According to this truth, they can do anything.

In family number two, the parents have created a good life for the family, but with a totally different perspective on life and with regards to themselves. They believe that you should be a bit cautious and not set your goals too high, as this can lead to disappointment. Perhaps this is because they have often been disappointed themselves.

One day, the son comes running towards his mother. He just turned four and his eyes are positively glowing with curiosity and a joy of living. With a big smile he tells her that: "I want to be a doctor!" His mother fidgets somewhat and replies: "That's difficult. Is there perhaps something else you want to do when you grow up?"

When he is eight, he has some new ideas. He wants to be a police officer, but is told that it is too dangerous. Later, he wants to be a scientist, have his own business, even become an astronaut, but each time he is told that it is very difficult and hard. Eventually, this becomes not only the parents' truth, but also their son's. Over and

over again, he is encouraged to dream about more common and realistic occupations. He is encouraged to lower his expectations in order not to be disappointed. Time and time again, they tone down their children's enthusiasm and eventually all of their children's dreams feel impossible.

Since they are told over and over again that their dreams are impossible to reach, a feeling is created saying that the dreams are unrealistic and unreachable. Not surprisingly, the children follow in the footsteps of their parents and settle down with more ordinary jobs.

All that the parents in the last example ever wanted was to see their children happy. They wanted to protect them. The question, though, is if they really became happier following in the safe footsteps of their parents than if they had followed their own dreams. The question is if they had been happier failing, while still having a sense of at least they gave it a shot.

These are just examples of how impressionable children are and how great a role their parents' values play in their lives. The parents in example two clearly did not mean any harm when they told their children that their dreams were more or less unrealistic. In these parents' worldview, these dreams were hard, but that does not mean that they would have been unrealistic or unreachable for their children.

There are a lot of good parents today. But sometimes it is a good idea as parents to stop and reflect on how we behave and what we really transmit to our children. How did I grow up? How did this affect me? Do I want my children to grow up the same way? Are we loving parents? Do we fight a lot? Do we encourage our children? Do we transmit our own limitations and problems unto our children? What kind of habits and routines do we have, and how do these affect our children? Everything children see and hear becomes their truth. They create their truths, which they then live by, perhaps for the rest of their lives.

A few years ago, I was travelling in the Bolivian countryside where I saw a donkey tied to a tree. Perhaps this does not sound all that extraordinary, but the rope used to tie the donkey was not all that thick. In fact, it was a sort of string that looked more or less like sewing thread. Naturally, I was curious as to why the owners did not tie up their donkey properly. It could have taken off at any time. Or could it? The owners explained to me that during the first year of the donkey's life, they used a thick rope to tie it to the tree, but now that it had stood there for many years, it did not know anything different. The donkey simply did not realize that it was able to move away from the tree.

I have later read about similar cases with animals from all around the world. Elephants being tied to small bushes or camels living in family backyards without leaving. Animals are also programmed with different kinds of truths, which they faithfully follow as long as they live.

Of course, there are exceptions. There are people who, for a number of reasons, choose not to be influenced by the truths of their parents. Swedish eighteenth century biologist Carl Linnaeus' parents, for example, wanted him to become a priest. This was probably because the father was a priest and thought that it had worked out fine for him. Carl did not listen to them and this troubled his parents. His teacher calmed them down by saying: "I'm sure he's going to be fine. He can always become a carpenter or something." Most of his teachers were annoyed by young Carl because he was so different, but there was one teacher who saw potential in him. He saw what interested the boy and he encouraged him. He often discussed flowers and plants with his pupil, who would later revolutionize the whole world with his theories about plant life.

Someone else who was seen by those around him as even being somewhat slow-witted was Albert Einstein. His childhood was difficult – it is even said that he did not learn how to speak until he was four. There was, however, someone who saw something completely different in the young boy and that was his uncle. He saw a great mind and when Einstein was five, he gave him a compass. The little boy became totally spellbound by the compass and this is where he set out on his journey to become one of the greatest minds in history.

It is hard to counteract how parents influence their children, but sometimes someone else may have such a strong influence on the child that his or her truths are completely changed and transformed.

Other kinds of truths may arise if, for example, you are bullied as a kid. Maybe you are teased for being fat, which in turn becomes a truth for you for a long time, even if you are not fat at all. When we come to a new workplace, it is common that we are extra curious and even start to question some things: "Why do you use this business software?" or "Why do you have these routines?" A common reply in these situations is: "That's just the way it is." We ask again: "But why?" We get no real answer, because our new colleagues live in accordance with the truth that "that's just the way it is." The company has certain routines and certain ways of doing things, but frequently no one really knows why. It has always been this way and it works. But the question is whether it would work better if something was changed.

There are a lot of examples of this in sports. If you play soccer or tennis, for instance, you are taught how to serve, curve the ball and move your body in the most efficient way. This, quite naturally, becomes your truth as long as you practice this sport. But what is to say that this particular technique is the best for you? Maybe it is the best for 95% of those who practice this sport, but is this technique really the best there is for you? Probably, it works out fine and you may even become very good at your sport, but maybe you could become even better if you swam against the tide and made a few changes.

Something that took place in the summer of 1968 comes to mind. It was time for the high jump finals during the Olympics in Mexico City. At that time, there were two techniques used by all athletes: the scissor and the straddle. When all the other jumpers warmed up, one man curiously enough did not make any trial jumps. His competitors must have wondered whether he was injured or whether he perhaps was hiding something. Maybe he had come up with something brand new? The competition started and Dick Fosbury stepped up and prepared himself for his first jump. He took off towards the bar, but just as he was about to jump, he turned around and jumped over the bar with his back towards the ground. The audience and all the experts were absolutely flabbergasted and two hours later the gold medal was his. Today, every single high jumper uses the same technique as Dick Fosbury.

Some people have the ability to not look at how other people do it, but to find their own ways. They find their own techniques or routines to succeed in sports, professionally or in their personal lives.

Everyone has their own truths based on upbringing, surroundings and experiences. Later in life, we subconsciously tend to recreate situations that remind us of our previous personal truths.

During a lecture I once attended in Vienna, the lecturer told us about a study showing that the most common reason for having children is because everyone else has them. We see our friends having children and are continuously told that this is how we should also live our lives. We need to peel off the impact of our childhood and our surroundings and ask ourselves what really is right for us. Maybe we have so many other dreams that we do not have room for children in our life. Sometimes we say things like: "The way they live, they shouldn't have any children." Maybe their child was not planned or maybe they decided to have kids just because everyone else has them. We should stop living our lives according to how the people around us expect us to live. We need to stop living like everyone else and instead listen more closely to our inner voice and follow our true self.

Imagine that you could reset your limitations to zero and get even more out of life by redrawing the blueprint of your own truths. Imagine that you could reset yourself to zero and, without being influenced by your surroundings, get a feeling of what really is true for you. I am convinced that we can alter our truths. I know that we, as adults, have the capacity to choose which truths to live by.

Whose truths do you live by? Are these truths correct or are they perhaps truths that were passed along to you? Are you happy with the truths in your life or do you wish that you were living according to a completely different set of truths? What if you are living according to false truths?

Let us pretend that you are ten years old and giving a presentation in front of your class in school. You are talking about something you really like, but your classmates are giggling. You get nervous, you get clammy and, while your face is turning red like a stop light, you begin to stutter. Your teacher walks over to you and encourages you by saying: "Take a few deep breaths and you'll see that everything will be OK." You get even more nervous and the whole class is now laughing at you.

After this incident, you are told that you are a dork. How would this affect you? Could new truths come out of a situation like that? Is it possible that this presentation leads you to create a new truth saying that you are bad at giving presentations? Could this truth in turn result in you feeling less confident talking in larger groups of people? Could it be that you begin to turn inwards and develop a fear of talking to certain people?

Imagine that this situation, when you were only ten, could have these kinds of consequences. Besides, you were not afraid to speak in front of the class. It was the giggling that made you insecure, and from this a truth was created that now says that you definitely do not like to speak in public. You do not like speaking in large groups and you are a quiet person, almost introverted. This, in turn, will guide your whole life – what line of work you choose, which friends you have, which hobbies and who you choose as a partner. A false truth has been created.

Everyone has false truths. And, by constantly questioning ourselves, it becomes easier for us to identify them. Ask yourself questions like: "Why do I get nervous or scared in some situations? What are my limitations or hang-ups?" Somewhere along the line, these truths were created. Find out where and when.

We can get pretty far simply by becoming more aware of the fact that we may have false truths, created years ago at some particular point in time. Stop, feel and reflect. Evaluate your life with a new perspective. Are you living the life you really want? Could it be that you have been influenced by those around you to live a life that is not completely yours? Ask yourself if you share some of your parents' habits. Do you share their values? Do you like the same things and live a similar life? Consider whether or not you sometimes think along the same lines as your parents and if this really is something you want. You may reach the conclusion that this is what you really want. Sometimes, however, we trick ourselves into believing that they are our own truths, when, in fact, they may be truths that were simply passed down to us.

Once you have identified which truths are your own and which truths are false or passed down, it becomes easier for you to see which ones are the best for you. It becomes easier to see which ones to keep and which ones to discard. Find out which truths you want to live by. Ask yourself: "Is it possible for me to live without these truths?" If the answer is no, then you need to ask yourself why.

Have you ever wondered why we sometimes answer: "No, I don't want to do that. That's not my thing. It's not me." Ask yourself why that's not your thing and why it's not you. Maybe you actually want it to be your thing. People tend to interpret thoughts about themselves and their surroundings as pure fact. That is why we perceive these truths as being real most of the time. In fact, our personality consists of nothing but a set of routine thoughts, emotions and actions. What this means is that we often create notions that do not correspond with reality. This is true regarding notions about ourselves as well as about our surroundings.

Sometimes we are told: "You can never do that" or "That's impossible!" Often, it is all too easy to listen to people saying that something is impossible, but it is important to understand why this person is telling you this. That is because his reasoning is completely different from yours. In his world, the truth is that it is impossible, but you live in a different world. Hopefully a world where it really can be done. Who says and who decides whether something is possible or not? You! You decide what is possible in your life. You, and no one else, decide what you want to change and how you want to live.

People who like to say: "That's not possible" have throughout their lives created a truth that this is the way things are. We have to accept that. They mean no harm. They just have a hard time realizing that there are many paths around the thick wall representing the obstacle. If you are told throughout your whole life that everything is difficult and risky, then that finally becomes a truth for you. But I promise you that it is never too late to modify a truth.

You can choose your own new truths. If you remind yourself of the new truths frequently enough, they become a part of your life. Never listen to people saying that something cannot be done. They do not decide what is possible for you. Make up your own mind as to what is realistically possible for you. Find the real reason for why something feels difficult. Try telling yourself that it is easy and accept the challenge to do that which previously seemed so hard. If it turns out to be simple, or at least less hard than you thought it would be, then you will know that it was a false truth.

"Your time is limited, so don't waste it living someone else's life. Don't be trapped by dogma – which is living with the results of other people's thinking. Don't let the noise of others' opinions drown out your own inner voice. And most important, have the courage to follow your heart and intuition. They somehow already know what you truly want to become. Everything else is secondary."

Steve Jobs

5
Your brain creates memory paths

You may think of thought patterns as going for a walk, but a walk taking place in your brain. If you take the same walk in the woods often enough, a path will be created. If you have the same thought a certain number of times, another path is created – a path in your brain.

When I am hiking in the woods, I always try to find the best places to walk. I want to get as much as possible out of my hike. The same is generally true in life. I want to get as much as possible out of it, which means that I should choose

which pathways I make in my brain with great care. In some places in the forest, it is very easy to create nice paths, whereas it is much more difficult in other places. Our brains work the same way.

I still remember playing a game of soccer when I was eight. The game was very close and with one minute left, we were up by 3-2. The other team was given a corner kick. I rushed back to help with the defense, the corner kick was taken and the ball came flying low towards me. Even thirty years later, I can still remember thinking: "Oh my! What do I do now?!" The ball hit my knee and bounced into my own team's goal. I scored an own goal and the game ended in a tie.

After this, I really came to hate corner kicks and my negative feelings about corner kicks linger still to this day. After this, I got worried every time I heard someone saying "corner kick." When the opposing team was about to take a corner kick, I always walked far up the field, covering some opposing player far away from my own goal. The risk of scoring another own goal was nil. This was a well-travelled path in my brain and I have very strong memories from this time. I remember smells, colors and disapproving faces. I also remember how I experienced the aggravation and frustration sweeping in like a huge hurricane over the soccer field.

I look upon our brains as having a plus and a minus account. Every negative experience is added to the minus account and every positive one is added to the plus account. Later, when we are faced with a new task, our subconscious mind asks itself: "Have I been through this before? Sure thing – I know corner kicks." And then I get terrified. Being aware of the fact that we have plus and minus accounts, it also becomes logical to try to make as many deposits into the plus account as possible, while trying to avoid minus deposits whenever possible.

In some situations, we are immensely self-confident, and that is because we have a very stable plus account in relation to these particular situations. These paths have been walked upon many, many times and we have been comfortable every single time. Have you noticed that some people seem to be comfortable all the time? They do not seem to have made any minus deposits at all. One person who comes to mind is Swedish soccer star Zlatan Ibrahimovic. He may miss a penalty kick during a game while 50,000 people are booing and some yelling things like: "You suck!" I think that a lot of people would find it hard to take a penalty kick after something like that. But the next time Ibrahimovic is about to take a penalty kick, he looks completely calm and unfazed. He has no problem whatsoever kicking the ball exactly where he wants it to go. The difference between him and others is that he chooses not to make a deposit into his minus account.

The spooky thing about our minus deposits is that they start out as small seedlings, but throughout the years they grow and may sometimes grow into large bushes or even massive, tangled shrubberies. We have to confront and deal with our fears. We have to stand face-to-face with something that frightens us a certain number of times to realize that it is not dangerous. I do not know about you as a kid, but I could every once and in a while convince myself that there was a ghost in my closet. I challenged this fear with the help of my mother. She would grab me by my hand, open the closet door and say: "Look, there are no ghosts here." I was still not convinced, so we would step into the closet together to take a look. In this way, I was convinced that there was no ghost. My fear disappeared. In our lives as adults, the fear could be speaking in public, realizing a dream, visiting the in-laws, going on a date, talking about our feelings and so on.

The most powerful memory paths are created in connection with strong emotions. Do you remember your first day in school? Do you remember a particular triumph or defeat? Do you remember when you fell in love for the first time? Even though these things took place years ago, you probably still remember them, since this type of experiences are connected to really powerful emotions.

Imagine a life with no fears or hang-ups and with total peace of mind. Imagine having the courage to make your life dreams come true, while, at the same time, being confident that you will succeed. I am convinced that it is possible, but we need to work on our thought patterns in order to get there. We need to let the unpleasant paths in our brains become overgrown with vegetation and we need to create new and delightful paths.

Our fears are created somewhere. Those afraid of speaking in public may have experienced something unpleasant in connection with giving a speech earlier in life. Without giving it much thought, they have avoided these kinds of situations throughout the years, while not really troubling themselves as to why. Furthermore, they have not considered if they want to or can do something about their fear of speaking in public. Often, you just think that this is the way things are, but I can assure you that there is more to it than that. There is a reason and you can do something about it.

Have you considered why some people are extremely good at certain things?

The excellent dancer, the fantastic cook or the great guitar player. These people have probably devoted a great deal of time on their particular skill and that is how we work. If we do something often enough, we will most likely become really good at it. The same goes for thought patterns. If, for instance, we tend to blame ourselves as soon as we do something bad, then we will eventually become really good at doing just that. We drop a glass and cry out: "Typically me – always the big klutz…" We are playing golf and end up in the woods: "I'm just terrible at this." If, on the other hand, we do something good in the kitchen or hit the golf ball straight as an arrow, we tend to neglect giving ourselves kind and positive feedback. Eventually, we become experts at filling our minus accounts. There is nothing strange about that, as we have walked along this particular path so many times before. Meanwhile, the pathways towards our plus account are starting to get brushy, or perhaps even getting to be completely overgrown.

Even if we are used to having certain thought patterns, it is possible for everyone to change the way they think. If we stop walking along a path, it gets overgrown. If we choose new directions, new paths are created. The new direction may be very hard in the beginning. The grass is tall, you get dirty and things are rough. But for each time you walk along this path, the easier it will get. You drop a glass in the kitchen, but what does it really matter? All you have to do is to clean it up and no great harm has been done. So what if you hit your golf ball deep into the woods? The next time it will get right onto the green and when it does, I think you should tell yourself how great you are. Make a fist and say "Great!" to yourself. This will be a deposit into your plus account.

There are many situations in life where you deserve praise. Give yourself a new habit to praise yourself whenever you do something good. Why do you think athletes make a fist when they do something good? Try making a fist when you do something good in your everyday life. Athletes do this because it gives them a positive and encouraging feeling, which in turn improves their chances of being successful in the future.

Our thought patterns create memory paths. The strongest paths are created when all of our senses are involved. I still clearly remember when I was eight, the corner kick was taken and I happened to kick the ball into my own team's goal. I remember people booing, I remember the smell of grass and, first and foremost, I remember how I felt – the bitter feeling of failure.

These days, I only play soccer every other year or so, but my fear of corner kicks is so deeply rooted that it is still there to this day. Every time the other team is about to take a corner kick, I take a deep breath, encourage myself and tell myself: "This is going to be OK."

Someone once said: "Choose your feelings just as you choose your clothes." Perhaps it is not that simple, but with patience we may be able to learn how to choose the right feelings. If there is something that easily creates bad feelings, then we can get to the bottom of as to why. If we know why, then we can do something about it. We can be conscious about the drawbacks of minus deposits. We can evaluate and think: "I am pretty good after all." We can stop saying that we are bad when we fail at something and instead compliment ourselves when we succeed. We can observe ourselves with kind eyes and see how beautiful we really are. We can look at ourselves and come to the realization that we are worth nothing but the absolute best.

No one else picks your thoughts – you are the only one who gets to decide what to think.

6
Create plus in your brain

For each plus deposit you make, the better you get at dealing with adversity. Minus deposits, on the other hand, damage your brain.

For every negative feeling passing through your body, you make a minus deposit and for each positive feeling, you make a plus deposit. Years ago, I used to coach tennis. My students were mixed in age – from 5 to 84. What they all had in common was that they all wanted to grow as players. To help them with this, we needed to work on their techniques, tactics, how to move and their mental framework. Strangely enough, a lot of my students had a hard time listening to my advice when all I did was telling them how to improve. When, on the other hand, I started out by complimenting them and then telling them what to improve upon, the criticism was more readily absorbed. When I only gave criticism, all the student heard was that he was bad.

Subconsciously, the student absorbed my criticism and made a deposit in the minus account. But when the student was first praised and then criticized, he realized that the criticism was a potential deposit in the plus account. Either we choose to put the negative experience into our minus account or we choose to see the experience as a potential plus deposit.

I do not actually remember the story I am about to tell you, but a few years ago my mother told it to me. When I was three, I looked up at my grandfather with a very curious look on my face and asked him: "Who decides what I should think?" My grandfather put his arm around my shoulder and said, reassuringly: "You do, my little friend. You decide for yourself what you think." Apparently, my reply was: "Boy, I'm lucky!"

Everyone runs into bad experiences once in a while. We all have our flaws, but the important thing is that we see these as something we can actually improve. If we really were unable to improve a single thing, then we would already be at the peak of our abilities, which, truthfully, would be quite dull. Some people have this perspective already programmed. They see flaws as something exciting and stimulating. They see the possibilities of becoming even better in their sports or professions, or even becoming better human beings. Others need to work a bit harder to face criticism, which in all actuality is a potential plus deposit. Perhaps they need to use the same method as in the case with the tennis players – praise followed by criticism. If there is no one around you giving you praise, then you can always give it to yourself. The advantage of praising yourself is that you can choose what you want to focus on. This may give you the energy to face your potential plus deposits.

The question is whether or not we sometimes judge ourselves too harshly. The fact is that it is a little bit too easy to focus on the criticism instead of basking in the warmth of praise. Let us say that you are playing a game of golf. You start by hitting ten really good shots followed by hitting the eleventh shot straight into the bush. The poor shot leads to a certain amount of irritation. Many times we sigh and say something like: "That shot of mine was awful." But wait a second! Before that, you hit ten really good shots. Shouldn't you have said: "That shot of mine was superb" ten times? Why do we choose to focus on the bad shot and not on the ten shots that were good?

For a few years I competed in something called racketlon. This is a fantastic sport where you face your opponent in four racket sports: table tennis, badminton, squash and tennis. As I was competing and travelling around the world, I became fascinated by one thing in particular. Some players had an incredible ability to perform well over their abilities. When the chips were down, they simply raised their level of performance to a level they really were not capable of.

This phenomenon can be seen in all kinds of top-level sports, and during my years in the world tour, I was trying to find out how this is actually possible. After studying a number of players, I concluded that people who often perform above their abilities primarily have two qualities in common. They are good at creating plus in their minds and they are exceedingly good at making withdrawals from their plus deposits.

Let me illustrate what I mean by giving you an example. A few years ago, I was watching a game between the third best ranked player in the world against a player ranked 280. The fact that the player ranked 280 should not have a snowball's chance in hell winning a game like this did not seem to face him at all. He kept making a fist, while constantly encouraging himself using phrases like: good play, awesome, great and come on. He was building up his plus account at a great speed. The third best player in world, however, was brooding over his poor performance. He really was not nice to himself. His minus account was rapidly growing. When the game was drawing to a close, the player ranked 280 exclaimed: "I'm fantastic and I'm about to win!" Meanwhile, he played incredibly well. The player ranked number three, however, played worse and worse.

After the game, I asked both players what they were thinking towards the end of the game. The player ranked number three told me that he thought about the dreadfully poor game he was playing. He had, in other words, dwelled on all the bad moves and mistakes he had made throughout the game. The player ranked 280, on the other hand, had focused on all of his good shots. When the game was reaching its final phase, he simply started to withdraw all the plus deposits he had made earlier in the game.

Have you considered that you can make yourself create plus in your mind by asking yourself the "right" questions? Instead of asking: "What did I do wrong during the game?" you can ask yourself: "What did I do well?" When you leave from work, you may ask yourself: "What have I accomplished today?" Before you go to sleep, you may ask yourself: "What was good about this day?" In the same manner, you can help the people around you to create plus in their minds.

Years ago, I had a colleague with a curious habit. He worked as a salesperson and when his clients were hesitant about signing a deal with him, he would frequently ask: "I hear that you are negative. What is it you find bad about our company?" The clients then proceeded to share with him what they did not like about the company. They proceeded to let the minus account grow.

I was assigned to motivate him to sell more. Once I asked him to think about what he usually asked his family when he came home from work. He thought about it for a long time and then said: "When I pick up my kids from daycare, I usually ask them if they have managed to avoid any trouble and then I ask them if it has been hard being away from me and their mother for the whole day." I listened to him quietly as he continued: "Later, when I come home to my wife, I almost always ask her if the problems at her job have been resolved or if it's still the same hardship as usual." He was completely unaware of how his questions affected those around him. He made his clients think about everything that was bad about the company and he made his children and wife think about problems and hardships. He, in other words, was helping the people around him to create minus in their brains.

It was obviously very hard for him to hear this, but a few months later he approached me and told me, with a smile on his face, that he had changed his questions. Talking to his clients, he would now say: "I hear that you find some things about our company negative, but tell me what you find positive." When picking up his kids from daycare, he would ask them: "So, what's the most fun that's happened today? What did you learn?" When he came home to his wife, he asked her: "What's the best thing that happened to you today?" He finished by saying: "My clients, my family and my friends, well, they all seem so much happier all of a sudden."

Imagine talking in front of 30 persons. Everyone seems interested and in good spirits, except for one person, who seems bored out of his mind. Should you focus your attention on the 29 persons who are actually listening, or should you focus on the single person who does not seem to be interested whatsoever? You just have to realize that everyone is different – we like and listen to different things. It could also be that the person looked like he was about to fall asleep because he was actually dead tired. It does not necessarily have to be that he was bored.

Imagine that your boss steps into your office and says that you are handling the billing very poorly. Consider how you process this information. What instructions are you giving your brain, which in turn guides your subconscious mind? Because that is exactly what you do. You are programming your feelings with the instructions you are giving your brain. It could be that you have 20 tasks you are supposed to do, and that billing is just one of these. As the boss seems to be very clear and straightforward, we can assume that you handle the other 19 tasks satisfactorily. There is only one task you need to get better at. I think you deserve to think: "I am really good at what I do, and now I am going to get better at billing."

If you fail in doing something – whatever it is – you have a choice when it comes to how you process this information. Either you choose to think: "I messed up. I am so ignorant" or you choose to think: "Alright, so I've made a mistake, but that's because I still haven't learned how to do it right. Now I know and I'll do better the next time around." No one else decides which choice you make – this is for you alone to decide. But keep in mind that the choice you make will affect and shape the structures in your brain.

In order to give ourselves the freedom to decide where to make the deposit, we sometimes need to prepare ourselves mentally. If, for instance, you are so nervous that you do not get your message across when giving a presentation to the board of your company, then this may lead to a large minus deposit. This could create problems for you in the future if you do not prepare yourself mentally that the next presentation you give will be a total success.

Most athletes put in a lot of effort in creating mental pictures of success. Using mental pictures is something we can all do. You can use these at work and in relation to situations you find hard. Mental images of success can be used when facing a challenge or if you are having a hard time believing that you will actually succeed in a particular task. When creating a mental image of this kind, sit down for a brief moment. Close your eyes and fantasize how you will succeed. For a few minutes, you let yourself imagine the success you wish for.

As commonly known, the brain is not capable of seeing the word "not." If I ask you *not* to think about a gorilla wearing a red bikini, what do you think you will end up thinking about? The same thing happens when you tell yourself that you can *not* fail, *not* make a fool of yourself, *not* make a mistake and other similar *not*-instructions. So, surely, it is much better to give the brain instructions on what to do, instead of what not to do. Imagine that you are going to the mall to buy clothes for your children. Your wife has been kind enough to write you a list, but only for things you are *not* to buy. Sounds confusing, I know, but it is just as confusing for the brain to deal with instructions for what we are not to do and what we are not to think.

The brain is built in such a way that it is constantly listening for instructions to follow – sort of like a computer. When you are sitting in front of your computer, you write commands for it to follow. If you write clearly enough, the computer will do what you ask it to. This is how your brain works too. You have the power over your brain. You are the one giving your brain instructions, which in turn affect your feelings and your subconscious mind. If you feed your brain positive items, you make it stronger. If you feed it negative items, you make it weaker.

7
How to create a new habit

The fact that we have a hard time breaking deep-rooted habits often stands in the way of us living the life we dream of.

Creating good habits is a prerequisite for feeling well. You need motivation if you want to create a good habit and discipline to break a bad one. We all have different habits depending on where we live. It is easy for a Swede, like me, to be amazed by how people around the world have the energy to work as much as they do. In Japan, for example, they only have nine days of vacation each year. Or we can look at poor countries in Africa, where some people are working up to 18 hours a day. Some of them are living under extremely harsh conditions – starvation, infections, physical pain, poor hygiene – but many are happy nevertheless. Frequently, we can see people with physical or mental disabilities displaying a greater sense of happiness and joy than those able to live completely normal lives. What is the key to this beautiful and genuine happiness? Why is it that the Japanese do not see their workload as an issue? What kind of a system are the African children using to be so happy? The simple answer: habits. It is all about habits.

Creating a new habit, or breaking an old one, takes a lot of effort. It is rarely sufficient to simply make up your mind to quit smoking, start exercising, be on time, live a healthier life or to be more positive. You have to work to accomplish this. Once you have gotten used to the new habit, it comes to you as naturally as getting up in the morning, eating breakfast, brushing your teeth or putting on makeup. Once you have made it a habit of yours to eat breakfast, you normally do not think: "Oh, what a drag, now I have to eat breakfast." You just do it, and it would take quite a bit for you to forget to eat breakfast.

A habit is born out of a feeling, a thought or in a specific setting, and habits include the routines you have made a part of your life. Some habits were passed down through your parents and some were created through your friends. Some habits have come to you through your job and some have consciously been made a part of your life. Others have subconsciously come to be a part of you.

Today, you have thousands of tasks you perform in your life without even thinking about them. This is because you have performed them so many times that you have taught the muscle memory in your brain to do them automatically. You run, walk, laugh, talk, stretch, get up, sit down, eat and drink. Before these became habitual activities, you had to learn how to do these things. This is how new habits are created. In the beginning, we need to be aware of how and when we want to use our new habit. Once we have repeated the habit a number of times, however, the brain's muscle memory takes over.

This is exactly how good habits are created, but also bad ones. All of our habits have been created through repetition, which eventually has taught the muscle memory to perform them automatically. Apart from having taught your muscle memory to perform habitual actions in your everyday life, at work and among friends, you have also taught it to automatically evoke certain feelings and to think in certain ways. Just like we can stop smoking and live healthier lives, we can also teach the muscle memory in our brains to induce certain feelings. We can also teach the muscle memory to stop having negative thoughts and instead have positive ones. The good thing about the muscle memory is that we can choose to keep habits that make us feel good and get rid of the ones that do not. Regardless of which habits, we can decide for ourselves which of these we want our muscle memory to perform automatically.

Studies show that 95% of all of your decisions are based on old habits. This means that only 5% of your decisions are conscious. This is kind of scary, considering that we are continuously changing and evolving, which in itself creates new needs.

When someone demonstrates a bad habit, we may hear something about "old habits die hard." That is true, old habits do die hard, but not just the bad ones. Our good habits also die hard.

Habits are also powerful in relationships, and sometimes it is possible for us to completely stop noticing particular habits. A few years ago, I was at a party given for a friend who turned 50. At my table, there was a couple in their 40s who had both developed an awful habit. He had made it a habit to constantly be mean and making fun of his wife, while she had gotten used to accepting this terrible behavior. Everybody around our table reacted to how badly he treated his wife, and finally I could not help myself and asked him how he could treat her this way. They both gave me an astonished look and wanted to know what I was talking about. Their deep-rooted habit, where she was constantly put down by her husband, was something they were completely unaware of. We never spoke of this again, but some years later I met the wife at a conference. She then told me that they had both been totally oblivious to how appalling his behavior really was. Then she looked at me with warm eyes and told me: "Now, he treats me with the utmost respect, because that is what I deserve."

Consider what kind of habits you have in your life and which ones you want to get rid of, or perhaps develop. This could be about sleep, exercise, eating sweets, cleaning, thought patterns or about the way you behave towards yourself and those around you.

Let us look at the nuts and bolts of creating a new habit.

Repetition, repetition and then some more repetition

It is a basic fact that we get better at the things we do frequently. Everyone who is good at something was once a beginner, but they have practiced, practiced and practiced, and have gradually gotten better and better at what they do. If you repeat something a certain number of times, a new habit (good or bad) is created.

Unfortunately, it is easy and quick to adopt bad habits like temptations, quick rewards, having negative thoughts and always preferring the path of least resistance.

The good habits, on the other hand, usually involve quite a bit more effort. A study shows that if a new routine is performed regularly, it takes on average 66 days to create a new habit. This study included habits like exercising or having a piece of fruit after lunch. There are also studies showing that if a new habit is particularly hard, then it may take up to 254 days to get used to it. Meanwhile, it takes on average 21 days to get used to a more simple habit. As you are trying to get used to a new habit, you will trip and fall in the beginning, but I can assure you that it will become easier over time.

All over the world, you may find trees and other plants that have miraculously survived for years under extremely odd and, in all fairness, impossible conditions. They have simply gotten used to living under these harsh conditions and that is how they survived. In the same miraculous way, we as humans can get used to most things.

Create an action plan

Before creating a new habit, you need to consider how you are going to adopt this new habit. Be specific about what kind of habit you want to create and what you think will assist you in this task. By adopting an action plan for how you are to make your new habit a part of your life, it becomes clearer where you want to go. Through your action plan, it also becomes easier for you to be patient and persistent.

Furthermore, if you put down your action plan on paper, you give yourself even more energy to start adopting your new habit. An action plan may be quite simple. Start by writing *which* habit you want to create, for example: "I want to live a healthier life."

Write down *how* you are to create your new habit: "I will exercise each Monday, Wednesday and Friday, and I will only eat sweets and drink alcohol on Saturdays."

Write down *why* you are creating your new habit: "I want to live a healthier life in order to feel better and to live longer."

Set up a time limit

During the process when you are teaching your muscle memory to adapt to the new habit, you will, from time to time, experience frustration. To make this process easier, you can set up a time limit for how long you are to actively teach your muscle memory. Knowing that there are only two weeks left, or a month, often gives you the power to keep it up.

Create an encouraging environment

Putting up little notes with kind and encouraging words will act as a reminder of your new habit and may also create motivation and energy. Let the people around you know that you appreciate positive feedback and, if that is lacking, give it to yourself. If, for instance, you are trying to get used to working out on a regular basis, you will get motivated and energized by hearing from people that they can tell you have been working out and perhaps even lost some weight.

You need to create routines for the new habit that work for you. But, nevertheless, you may become inspired by looking at how others with this particular habit do it. You may also spend time with those who have already embraced the habit you are trying to make your own. If, for example, you want to start exercising, then you may socialize with others who do so regularly. You will then be reminded of exercise and hopefully you will see their good results from exercising, which in itself may be very inspiring. Thus, quite naturally, you will most likely also get support and encouragement that helps keeping you motivated.

Also imagine the nice feeling once the new habit becomes a natural part of your life. Remember to focus your thoughts on what the new habit will mean to you. In this way, you will create the inner motivation necessary for making your new habit work in the long run.

Adapt gradually

When you want to adapt to a new habit, it may sometimes be easier to do this gradually. If you want to get used to getting up one hour earlier every morning, it may be a good idea to only get up earlier on Monday the first week, Monday and Tuesday the following week, and so on.

Create one new habit at a time

A very ambitious friend of mine once told me that she thought of herself as being bad at creating new and healthy habits for herself. I asked her how she goes about creating new habits. She told me that she usually creates action plans, in addition to writing down the habits she wants to adopt. But, nevertheless, she kept on failing. Her mistake was that she had tried to start 22 new habits, all at once. Concentrating on one habit at a time is in most cases easier than trying to create a number of new habits simultaneously.

Reward yourself

Motivate yourself further by creating a reward. We always deserve a reward when we succeed in the difficult task of creating a habit.

It is just as hard to start a new habit as it is to break an old one. Just as we can teach the muscle memory to remember a good habit, we can also teach it to forget an old one. But how do we actually break a bad habit? Well, we just trade one habit for another.

As there is almost always a void when you quit a bad habit, you need to fill this void by creating a new one. We simply replace the bad habit with a good one. If, for instance, you want to quit having cinnamon rolls with your coffee, then you just replace the roll with a whole-wheat sandwich. If you want to quit eating candy, then you switch out the candy to a healthier alternative. Selfish acts are replaced with altruistic ones. Stress is replaced with relaxing. Mean thoughts are replaced with kind ones. Watching too much TV may be replaced with reading a book. If you want to be an even better husband and not let your wife bear the brunt of your frustration, then replace your frustration with love. Likewise, you may replace the habit of having negative thoughts with having positive ones. If, for a certain amount of time, you constantly remind yourself to think positive thoughts, then your positive thought trails will become the most natural way for you to think. When you give your brain opposite inputs, it becomes impossible for the brain to use its muscle memory to perform acts in the way it is accustomed to. In this way, you compete with your bad habits. Try it the next time you are annoyed or feeling down. Try to act as if you are happy. Stand tall, smile and think the kind of thoughts you normally do when you are happy.

When you want to quit a bad habit, you need to consider how to give yourself the best chances of success. If, for example, you want to give up smoking, then there are many things you need to consider. How can you replace smoking? Maybe by exercising, making a dream come true or by reading books? If you spend time with friends who smoke, then you will constantly be reminded of how truly satisfying you, at this moment, consider a cigarette. Conversely, if you spend time with people who do not smoke, then you will be reminded of how a healthy life without smoking may look like.

Tell your friends and family how you believe your behavior will change during this transitional phase and ask for their support and understanding. Which methods should you use when you have the biggest craving for cigarettes? Deciding on which methods to use is individual, but a method that often works is scaring yourself towards change. Finding out what you will look like and how your health will deteriorate in 10, 20 or 30 years if you do not quit smoking will sometimes be so frightening that you will come to the conclusion that you have no other option but to quit.

A colleague of mine from a long time ago was very interested in fashion and dressing well. One day he showed up at work with clothes that were way too tight for him. His belly was about to tear his shirt open and his pants were so tight that he could not even close the top button. He really did not look at all comfortable in his new clothes.

Later in the afternoon, over coffee, he told me that he had tried to lose weight for a long time, without ever being successful. Now, he had found a new method where he forced himself to wear clothes two sizes too small. Being around others, he was embarrassed and the fact that he could barely move in his way too tight clothes was obviously a nuisance to him. I have hardly ever seen someone so motivated about losing weight. After seven weeks, his clothes fit him perfectly.

If you want to create a habit of getting up earlier in the morning, then a possible method could be to have a particularly good breakfast to look forward to, or perhaps an interesting newspaper to read with your breakfast. Hence, you have something extra to look forward to when the alarm goes off in the morning.

When you want to create a new habit, you need to put yourself in situations that automatically remind you of your new habit. If, on the other hand, you want to break a bad habit, then you need to put yourself in situations that do not remind you of this particular habit. The everyday settings are often crucial as to whether or not we will succeed in creating or breaking habits. The setting may force you to break a habit. If, for example, you want to stop eating fatty foods for lunch, then you may automatically break this habit by starting to go to a restaurant that only serves food lower in fat.

In the sixteenth century, the Spanish arrived with eleven ships on the beaches of what would later become Mexico. Their powerful leader Hernán Cortés ordered his men to burn their ships. They protested, but Cortés would not budge and made them set the ships on fire. Even though they were vastly outnumbered by their enemies, they now had two options: to die or to defeat the Aztecs. Since they had burned their ships, they no longer had any means of getting away. They could not give up now. They had to fight to their last breath and they had to focus all of their efforts and energy towards winning. It may seem as if Cortés' plan was somewhat ill-conceived, but this was not the case. It was a carefully thought-out tactic, where he first collected their food and other supplies before setting the ships on fire.

When we create new habits, we need to eliminate potential escape routes. If, for instance, you want to start working out, it is easy to end up in a swamp of excuses about not having the time or being too tired. By creating more time and by getting enough sleep, you eliminate your escape routes for avoiding exercise. My colleague who was wearing clothes that did not fit him had eliminated his escape routes by throwing out all of the clothes that fit his current size.

Another way of putting a little bit more pressure on yourself is to tell the people around you about your new habit. That usually makes it harder to escape. If you block your escape routes, you may no longer seek them. Thus you make it much easier for you to only focus on how to create or break your habit.

When people go through life-changing tragedies, like losing both their legs, it is understandable that their first thought is that their life is over. Miraculously, though, most people struggle to regain their lives. Once again life is coming along nicely, but now with a disability and perhaps in a wheelchair. How did this happen? That they were able to return to life, and sometimes with an even stronger will to live than before?

Clearly, they get a brand new perspective on life, but this is also about the ability to adjust life to their new circumstances. These kinds of adjustments can be made by creating new habits. These people do not have any escape routes either. There are no excuses and there is only one alternative – to get back to life and live it as normally as possible. I see those who struggle to get back to life after a tragedy as great heroes, but I am also convinced that there is a hero inside each and every one of us. Imagine if we had the courage to release our inner hero to change our old habits. The fact of the matter is that you can change your habits on all levels of life, including how you think and feel. Apart from the fact that your new habits make you feel better, you also increase the likelihood of reaching your full potential as a human. Your life becomes easier and better with good habits. And, at the same time, new habits stimulate your brain in an incredibly positive way.

Finally, I am wondering how the children in the poorest countries in Africa really manage to stay happy, despite their terribly harsh living conditions. Most likely, these children have subconsciously created a habit of focusing on what they have in life instead of focusing on what they are missing. If my theory is correct, then that would mean that happiness comes from the inside – not from the outside in the shape of money, nice cars or grand homes – but through the ability to accept and appreciate one's current position in life, no matter what it looks like.

I wonder whether the best habit in the world is being kind and loving those around you. Or is the best habit in the world looking for the good things in life?

8
Create magic by using goals

When driving a car you need a destination, or else you will never get there. When you are walking in the deepest of forests, you need some kind of compass to be able to navigate. In life, your goals serve as your guide. They serve as an inner compass and help you navigate through life to where you want to go.

Very few things in life are free. Almost all of us have to struggle to get what we want. Goals create energy and the power of working with goals is magical. Nevertheless, there are many people who never give themselves goals. A common reason is that they have not yet realized the power of using them. A lot people are also afraid of failing to achieve their goals. Reaching a target is difficult. A number of factors determine whether it will end in success or in failure.

Inner motivation

A lot of people say that they are bad at achieving their goals. But, most of the time, this is not about them being bad at achieving their goals, but rather that they lack the right motivation. You are trying to decide whether to accept that status-filled job and make loads of money, or whether to take the job at the coffee shop where you can bake and dedicate yourself to your passion. Your family and your friends may say: "Of course you should take the job that gives you status and money." Just because the people around you focus on their careers does not necessarily mean that this should automatically also become one of your goals. You may want to achieve completely different goals. Sometimes we give ourselves goals we believe to be our own, while it is in fact those around us who expect us to have these goals (see chapter 4).

A basic prerequisite for reaching a difficult target is that it comes from within yourself. You need to understand why you want to achieve this goal so badly. So, simply find out what truly motivates you to achieve this particular goal. Then you will find the core of your inner motivation.

Goal-benefit-meaning

To find the core of your inner motivation, I have developed a simple method, which I refer to as the GBM-model. This means that you initially have a clear goal. You completely understand the benefits of reaching this goal and you understand the meaning of succeeding. Understanding the meaning of reaching the target is the core of your inner motivation. You may use this model to achieve all kinds of goals, for example:

Goal: To create a better work environment.
Benefits: The staff members feel better.
Meaning: The staff will be more loyal, work more and the company becomes more profitable.

Goal: Building a tree house for your daughter.
Benefits: Your daughter gets fresh air and has fun playing in her new tree house.
Meaning: The fact that she is getting fresh air and having fun makes her happy and feeling good.

Goal: Travel the world.
Benefits: Fantastic experiences, adventures and relaxation.
Meaning: You evolve, get inspiration and energy while growing as a person.

Goal: Cleaning out the closet.
Benefits: Having a clean closet, in addition to everything being where it is supposed to be.
Mening: You will have an easier time finding things, which will make your life easier.

Goal: Starting an exercise regimen.
Benefits: Social interactions plus getting in shape.
Meaning: Improved health, more energy, getting stronger and living longer.

Goal: Improving your financial situation.
Benefits: You can pay your bills on time, can afford to eat better and can afford more of the good things in life
Meaning: More freedom, less stress, improved health and more joy.

Specific and concrete goals

Try to create as concrete goals as possible. The better you can specify your goals, the easier it will be to achieve them. If your ultimate goal is to become a better parent, then you need to be concrete as to which of your qualities as a parent you wish to work on. It is not enough to simply say that your goal is to be more present as a parent. You need to find out exactly what it is you want to develop in order for you to be more present, like being a better listener, becoming more involved in your children's interests, working less while at home, showing even more love or going on more family trips.

When it comes to some goals, it is also helpful if they can be measured. The clearer the goals you set, the easier it will be to get measurable results that will motivate you.

Write down your goals

Giving yourself goals without putting them down on paper are usually wasted goals. Some scholars even say that goals do not exist until they are written down. Writing down our goals is a good way to clarify them and to get some structure. By writing down your goals, you are reminded of what you want to accomplish. You supply more momentum and the goals are etched into your conscious thoughts, which helps you to focus your attention in the right direction. In this way, you create a filter that automatically blocks out the things that are not important to you.

During an experiment at Harvard Business School, it turned out that only 3% of the participants were used to having clear goals, written down on paper, in addition to having action plans for achieving these. Ten years later, a follow-up study was carried out, showing that this group of 3% made ten times as much money as the remaining 97% did combined. It was argued that the only real difference between the two groups was their approach to working with goals.

Rephrase goals you previously failed to achieve

If we have previously failed to achieve a certain goal, it is easy to once more fall into the pattern of failure if we go about it the same way as before. If you previously had the goal of losing weight, and failed, then you may rephrase your goal to eating better and exercising more, which, in turn, will make you drop pounds.

Create timeframes

Something else that helps you reach your target is to create timeframes. You need to have an idea as to how long you will have to struggle to achieve a goal. It is easy to delay your journey towards the goal if you do not feel any time pressure. Some goals are nothing but fun, but sometimes we face goals that feel more challenging, and this is where it feels good to have a timeframe. If, for example, you are working on a project at work that takes up a lot of time and energy, then it could be good for you to know that you will have reached your goal in two months. This also creates a sense of positive stress, which, in most cases, makes your efforts even more focused.

Schedule some targets

Most people who are successful when fulfilling goals set aside time when to work out, play the guitar, write a novel, study or work with their own business. When we set aside time for our goals, we create a long-term approach.

Visualize your goals

And now we get to one of the corner stones of using goals – visualization. Every time you see your goal, something happens inside of you. Because every time you see your goal, it grows stronger, becoming more alive and this is exactly when it happens. It starts to work for you. By writing down your goals and putting them somewhere visible, you get a very powerful reminder that will fill you with energy and inspiration day after day. The more often you are reminded of your goals, the stronger your motivation to achieve them will be. And, with time, you will subconsciously steer your decisions towards your goals.

On our journey, we sometimes face resistance, but the feeling of wanting to give up must not overcome us. When you are in the middle of a long uphill walk, it is easy to experience frustration and fatigue, and it is precisely at this point when you need to be reminded of what awaits you at the top of the hill.

Just like you may visualize work-related goals, you may also visualize goals related to your personal growth. A good friend of mine thought long and hard about how to visualize his goals. He considered himself to be too negative and this was something he wanted to change. He really understood the importance of visualization and he had carefully written down his intermediate goals of how to become a more positive person. For a long time, he tried different ways to visualize his goals. He tried writing them on his fridge, on his bathroom mirror, on his desk and in his car, but he needed a more powerful spot for his visualization. Then he realized that he had to go to sleep and wake up with his intermediate goals. So he did. His method of visualization was complete and the next night, before going to sleep, he read out his intermediate goals. They were all carefully written down and the spot he had picked for his visualization was his bedroom ceiling. Two months later, his negative thoughts existed no more.

The magic of using intermediate goals

If we want to succeed in working with goals, then they need to be relevant. You must feel that it is actually conceivable for you to reach them. Something almost all athletes have in common is that they are very good at working with intermediate goals. If a golf player has the goal of becoming the best player in the world, then she often breaks down this goal into a number of smaller intermediate goals, like, for instance, that she will be in the top 100 within six months, in the top 50 a year from now, and so on.

Even individual competitions are often broken down into a number of smaller goals. Those who are very good at racket sports, for instance, often have the intermediate goal of just winning one point at a time. If a player with a world ranking of 200 meets the player ranked number one, it is easy to get the feeling that it is impossible for him to win. The goal is simply way too distant to be realistic. If, however, he breaks down the game into small goals like: "I am going to win this point," a much more realistic feeling is created. He also knows that if he wins "this point" enough times, he will win the game.

A great feeling is created when we achieve a goal that matters to us. If we break down long-term and difficult goals into a number of smaller intermediate goals, then we will get to experience this great and energy-boosting feeling of reaching a target more often. This, in turn, fuels our desire to reach even more targets. If you are to run a marathon, then the thought of having 26 miles ahead of you may feel tough. Instead, break down the race into a few smaller goals, like the first water stop and the first five miles.

If your goal is to overcome your fear of speaking in public, then you may give yourself smaller goals. For instance, that you are to tell a joke to your friends within a week's time, that you are to tell the same joke to all your co-workers in three weeks, that you will give a speech in front of a video camera in six weeks and, finally, give a practice speech in front of your family in ten weeks. Your actual, final goal may be something along the lines of giving a speech at the big family reunion.

There are also physiological benefits when working with intermediate goals. Our brains are built to love quick rewards. According to Swedish brain scientist Katarina Gospic, this is because the brain perceives quick rewards as bigger than the long-term ones. When we reach an intermediate target, the neurotransmitter dopamine is released. If the goal is too far off in the future, or unrealistic, our reward signals do not work and the goals lose their powerful effect.

For each intermediate goal, you get a reminder that you are approaching your final goal. Meanwhile, a sense of encouragement is created, giving you even more power to reach the next target. Working with smaller intermediate goals in order to gradually get closer to the final goal is similar to the way different kinds of phobias are treated. Someone suffering from ophidiophobia (fear of snakes) may first start to cure this phobia by simply talking about snakes, then looking at pictures of snakes, followed by looking at a live snake, in order to, finally, having worked up the courage to actually touch a snake. Sometimes a goal may feel absolutely impossible. We see in front of us an enormous mountain of tasks we have to complete in order to achieve our goal. But, if we choose to look at this mountain as a pile of smaller stones, then it becomes so much easier for us to focus on one stone at a time. The feeling of then seeing the mountain becoming smaller and smaller with each stone we take away will give us even more energy.

Create an action plan

A study shows that 90% of all New Year's resolutions are broken, in spite of us being certain that we will succeed. The most common reason is that we lack an action plan. You need to have a plan to be certain that you will reach your goal.

Reaching a goal at work may involve you finding out who to include, how much time you need to dedicate and which steps you need to take in order to succeed. If you have a goal to go to the gym regularly, then you need to decide which days and times you are to go. You need a workout routine that fits you and it may be a good idea to know how long it will take for you to complete your whole routine. You need to consider how to make it more long-term and what you need in order to keep your motivation come summer, when you know that you want to spend a lot of time outdoors. Maybe you need to go to the gym together with a friend to keep your long-term motivation, or perhaps you need to find a routine at the gym you really, really like. Whatever goals you have, you need an action plan telling you how to get there.

Reward yourself

It is possible that your inner motivation and understanding of the meaning of achieving your goal is a reward in itself. Nevertheless, on your journey towards the goal, you will most likely end up experiencing resistance and frustration. In these cases, you need to be strong and focus on a reward in order to be able to carry on. Your reward to yourself could be something like going on a trip or to a spa, buying that coat you have been checking out or having a day off work. Other possible rewards could be to give yourself more time to pursue your interests or maybe even giving yourself more time to pick up a new one.

Spending more quality time with your family, being outdoors or having a really nice dinner may also be energy-boosting rewards. The musts of our everyday lives get so much more manageable if we know that we will get a reward. If you have to clean out your closet, cut down a tree or paint your house, then it helps if you throughout all of this hard work remind yourself that you will have a small reward once the work is done – perhaps a nice dinner, a cold beer or getting to soak it up in the bathtub.

Create a mental image of success

To reach a difficult goal, you also need to be mentally prepared. Scholars say that the brain is constructed in such a way that it thinks in images. This means that it will be beneficial for you to create positive goal images before trying to achieve a target. You could also say that the brain is set to do everything twice: first conceptually and then in reality.

When you create a mental image of success, you close your eyes for a few minutes. Imagine that sweet feeling you will experience when you succeed, and then imagine what this success will mean to you. Open your eyes. You are now ready to embark on your journey towards your goal.

Flexible goals

A lot can happen trying to reach your goal. You may discover that you get more inner motivation if you change your goal somewhat, or you may notice that it takes longer than you calculated. Being flexible, we are able to tweak our goals and therefore get even closer to our inner wishes.

Update your goals

If you have a job where the goals are more or less the same month after month, then chances are that the goals will become less powerful over time. For your goals to give you power, you need to update and change them every once in a while. The brain's reward system reacts to new things, which means that the goals are much more efficient when you make small changes or spice them up.

Evaluate your goals

Once you have achieved a goal, ask yourself: "How well did I succeed in reaching my goal? What did I do well and what can I do better next time?" If you reach your goal very easily, then you need to consider whether you should give yourself a more challenging goal the next time around. Evaluating your goals gives you the opportunity to make the kind of fine adjustments that will make you even better at achieving your goals in the future.

Your life vision

Albert Einstein once said: "When you fantasize about the future, you get a glimpse of things to come."

Everyone needs a life vision. Your vision works as your inner roadmap and it will consciously, as well as subconsciously, help guide you through life. If you have a clear vision of the future, then you can also set the targets that will steer you in the right direction. In other words, what do you want your life to look like in 3, 5, 10, 20 and 40 years? What kind of a vision do you have professionally and in your private life? Where do you want to live in the future? Which interests do you want to have and how much leisure time will you have at your disposal? What does your ideal life look like? What do you have to do today to be able to give yourself a reasonable chance of fulfilling your life visions? Which goals do you have to set for yourself? Which decisions do you have to make? Which steps do you have to take? If your life vision is to spend your time in a cottage in rural France when you turn 55, then you need to start planning at this very moment for how you are to reach this goal financially. You will also be able to absorb valuable information that may be useful when you finally leave for Provence or Brittany.

I frequently hear people talking about their visions. Some want to travel the world when they retire, others want a house in Spain. These visions are good in themselves, but a lot of people forget to create an action plan for how they are actually going to fulfill these visions. If you want to fulfill your visions, then you need to have a clear plan for how to reach them and even set time limits for the smaller steps, which turn into intermediate goals.

You need to constantly remind yourself of your life visions, which means that you have to visualize them. Make them visible – preferably somewhere where you are reminded of them daily. Why not the fridge? Every time you open your fridge, you will be reminded of the direction of your life. If you get reminded frequently enough, it will eventually become your reality, and this is exactly how we also work when it comes to our visions.

The purpose of making your life visions clearer and to visualize them is that you will then subconsciously steer your decisions towards your visions. Your subconscious mind will eventually guide many of your life choices and the visions will also guide your goals. Before you know it, you are going in exactly the direction you want. The vision is crucial for your life to evolve in the direction you dream of. The more the vision is making itself heard, the quicker you will get there.

"Tell me your vision and I will tell you your future."

Yonngi

9
Resist temptations

The Dalai Lama once said: "The true secret on the road to happiness is commitment, effort and time."

One of the greatest traps, by far, for making us feel bad is when we fall for different kinds of temptations. There are thousands of temptations in your life and we may all fall for these. Here are a few examples: Being tempted to break a good habit or to avoid a necessary argument. The temptation to have negative thoughts or letting someone else bearing the brunt of your frustration. The temptation not to resist greed or to buy things even when we cannot afford them. Being tempted to eat that bag of sweets or having another glass of wine, even though we really should not. The temptation of spending time with people who have a negative influence on us, or being tempted to constantly wanting more and more of the good things in life.

On your journey through life, you may meet many enemies and the most dangerous ones are often temptations. These enticements are future threats, but there are many things you can do preventatively to help yourself steer away from them.

Practice self-control

Have you considered what actually happens when you fall for a temptation? Could it be that it sneaks up on you when you least expect it?

A regular, unremarkable afternoon, a friend of mine fell for the temptation to skip going to the gym that day. Just once does not make a difference, right? The weeks passed by and he skipped going to the gym more and more frequently, and now, a year later, my friend is 30 pounds heavier and has not been to the gym in nine months.

Many years ago, a colleague of mine told me that she had bumped into an old childhood friend in the city. She was really happy about this and she told me that they were going to have lunch together some day. As she was positively glowing when she told me about her childhood friend, I asked her if she had ever had a crush on him. She told me that she had, and she also told me that he had been her first crush ever. The weeks went by and they started to see each other more and more. One Friday they were planning to go out and have a glass of wine. I asked her how this new friendship affected her marriage. No problem, she said, she was in total control of the situation. But, as it turned out, the lunch led to a walk, the walk led to dinner, the dinner led to going out for drinks and eventually they both fell for forbidden temptations. Temptations resulting in divorce and misfortune.

I would say that there are two different ways of resisting all kinds of temptations in life. The first is to teach ourselves to steer clear of the temptation by acting preventatively. The second way is to practice self-discipline, so that we learn to control the things that tempt us.

There are many ways to effectively build self-discipline. One very simple method is to buy your favorite chocolate bar. Leave it in your kitchen throughout the week. It is OK to look at it, but you are not allowed to eat it until Saturday.

Another method for practicing self-discipline is to do something you really do not care for. It could be working out for 30 minutes or shutting off your e-mail or phone for a while. When you expose yourself to things you do not like, you feel more disciplined and this strengthens your sense of self-control. If you prefer to sleep for ten hours every night, then you may build self-discipline by only sleeping eight hours. If you strive for perfection, then you may practice reducing your need to be seen as perfect. If you are tempted by negative thoughts, then you may build self-discipline by deciding to forbid yourself from having these thoughts at certain times.

The next time you are tempted, find out the price of that temptation. Ask yourself: "If I fall for this temptation, what does that mean to me and my life? How will I feel if I fall for this temptation and how does this affect my life and well-being?"

Being blind in your everyday life

Living a structured life, we may work less and "live" more. Most people waste a lot of unnecessary time and energy due to the simple fact that they do not know where all of their time is really going. Did you know that, on average, you lose 30% of every normal workday to incoming e-mail and telephone calls?

This is due to the fact that when we have to quit the task at hand, we will then need some starting-up time to get back to the level of concentration required for that specific task. We are each and every day tempted to check incoming e-mails and answer phone calls. We are constantly tempted to help out friends and colleagues, even though we often do not have the time.

Since we are often blind to our own habits and behavioral patterns, it is sometimes good to analyze how all of our time is spent. Make a time analysis to really find out how you spend your time. Once you have found an everyday structure where you do not waste unnecessary time, you will cut down on stress and also get more time to do the things that truly matter to you.

Ask yourself what it would mean to you and your life if you could find enough structure to make your days 20% more effective.

A lot of people I talk to say that they barely have enough time to get their work done due to all the cold calls from people trying to sell them things. Create a certain time slot for all the sales calls. Simply refer everyone who calls you to this time slot. Also, create certain time slots for the company's internal meetings. Some people say that they find it hard to get their work done due to all internal meetings. Ask yourself if you really have to participate in every single meeting and if these really have to be so time-consuming. Have the courage to ask yourself if you are really focusing on the right things and if you really reach the goals of all of your meetings. Have the courage to delegate – you do not have to be in total control when it comes to everything. Sure, you may know how to do these particular things better than anyone else, but let others learn how to do them in order to give you time to do other things.

Trying to be more effective at work, perhaps you can inform your colleagues that the hours of 8-12 a.m. every day is your so-called "prime time." During these hours, you need to work totally uninterrupted and without questions and conversations. During this time, you only take truly pressing phone calls and only answer urgent questions. You may also try closing your inbox and shutting off your phone at certain times.

We also need to get really good at prioritizing. How often do we end up saying: "I don't have the time and I have way too much to do." The next time you hear yourself utter these words you know that you have prioritized things incorrectly.

I promise you that by using good planning and getting your priorities right, you may free up additional hours every day. Yes, you read it correctly – additional hours each and every day.

It is said that we spend 20% of our time on the things that really matter to us. Every one of us wastes more time than we are aware of. Try to figure out where you are wasting time and carry out the changes at work and in your day-to-day life that are feasible.

Consider how you may change your routines in order to get more time for the things that matter the most to you. Try resisting the temptation to do what everyone else is doing, and also try resisting the temptation to keep doing the things you have always done. If you want to get up at four in the morning to have a cozy morning with your husband – then do so. If you want to take some time off work in the middle of the day to write a love letter to your wife – then do so. If you hesitate, ask yourself the following: "If I do not take time off work, then my boss may be happy, but if I take an hour off to write my wife a love letter, then she will be happy. What is the most important to me?"

Planning and having structure in our everyday lives means that we create more time to do the things we really treasure.

The powerful word "no"

Sometimes it is very hard to say no. And, even when we shouldn't, we are sometimes tempted to say yes; if only to prevent ourselves from disappointing someone. Some time ago, a friend of mine told me that he was very frustrated about his life being so fully booked and inflexible. As he did not have any children, I was especially curious as to what took up so much of his time. He replied that every weekend for the next six months was already fully booked with dinner parties with his family or with other couples. At the same moment he said: "There are quite a few of these dinner parties that neither one of us – my girlfriend and I – want to go to." I replied: "Do you really think that your relatives and friends want you to come, even though the two of you really don't want to?" He stared at his feet and was silent for a little bit. Then he looked me in the eyes and, with a little smile on his face, he said: "Sometimes it may be more polite to both myself and to my friends if I learn to say no every once in a while."

One summer, when I was 20, I was working in a margarine factory. One day, I was riding around the factory on my pallet lifter when I spotted a co-worker hiding behind two big boxes. I approached him and just when I was about to ask him if everything was OK, he made a shush sign, signaling to me to be absolutely quiet. A minute or so later, he grabbed my arm and said quietly: "Let's split!" Every Friday afternoon he apparently went through this ritual and his goal was to hide from the factory foreman. This was his method to avoid having to work overtime during the weekend. He simply found it so hard to say no that he would rather play hide-and-seek with the manager.

If you frequently find yourself in situations where you end up saying yes, even though you do not want to or do not have the time, then you should start practicing saying no. I suggest that you start saying no in more trivial situations, where your no is not that significant. After that, you can go on to say no if you do not want to work overtime or attend dinners. Saying no is about showing yourself respect, and the only one who can set your boundaries is You.

The skyscraper model

When I was 19, I lived in the US for a period of time, more specifically in Mesa, Arizona, and I can still remember how fascinated I was with all the skyscrapers in the big cities. I simply could not fathom how it was possible to construct buildings a thousand feet high that could withstand hurricane strength winds. During bad storms, someone told me, a skyscraper may sway as much as three feet. While in New York City, I visited a worksite where they were building yet another skyscraper. I asked how they actually manage to get balance and stability in these tall buildings. One of the contractors told me that the first thing you need is a really good and stable substructure, but he also told me that this is not enough in bad weather. In order to be able to beat bad storms, you need to construct a number of so-called spread footings and supporting columns, which work together to support the buiding through high winds. He told me that they were using six spread footings in this project and that these combined provided the building with enough balance and stability. He also told me that there would be a great risk of this skyscraper falling down if they were only to use two or three spread footings.

So, how do we translate the skyscraper model to our daily lives? To have good balance in your life and to be able to stand firmly in strong winds, you also need a number of spread footings or, shall we say, foundation stones. These could be your

family, a rewarding job, a peaceful home, great friends and stimulating interests. Sometimes, though, we are tempted to disregard this balance and this is when we risk falling down or even crashing. An acquaintance of mine once told me that she no longer needed anything else in her life apart from her great husband and their children. I asked her if she did not miss her friends or the interests she used to enjoy. She answered that her husband and her children gave her everything she could ever dream of, so she did not think she needed anything else.

A few years later, I ran into her once again, but I had a hard time recognizing her at first. She looked as least 15 years older. She had lost that happy twinkle in her eyes, as well as her warm and friendly smile. She told me that she and her husband had separated a year earlier, and that this was when her whole life fell apart. With a sad, but insightful voice she said: "I never really understood what you were talking about when you told me about all of these foundation stones being necessary for having balance and stability, but now I know what you meant." When we build our life on a number of different foundation stones, we create a healthy balance and a strong substructure for our lives. This helps us to stand firmly when we experience strong winds. If we have more legs to stand on, we are not as vulnerable when we lose our job or face tragedies.

The famous balance in life is just as important to us as having a balanced diet, exercising and sleeping well.

Some reflections on keeping it simple

I understand that outer success may sound appealing. A well-paid and prestigious job, a cool car, clothes that signal success, money, a nice beach house, a motorboat and travelling to exotic destinations. But is there a downside to outer success?

If you have ever been lucky at a casino, then maybe you have suffered from the temptation of wanting even more. If you have not suffered from this temptation, then you have probably seen someone else becoming a victim of this phenomenon. This is a trap many people fall into in their daily lives. Many years ago, I had a conversation with a man who had an abundance of material things. His descendants would not have to work for a couple of generations. He said it like this: "Before I had more money than I could spend and all of these things, I was extremely jealous of those who did. I imagined that if I could just get really, really rich, then my life would be better. Now I've gotten used to having all of this, but my life is still not better and I don't feel the least satisfied. Instead, I just want more." This man lived together with his wife and their three nice kids. He had also recently become a grandfather. I asked him if he could at least experience some kind of happiness sometimes: "No," he said, "I feel completely empty and nothing makes me happy anymore."

This man had clearly achieved outer success, but, unfortunately, he had failed in achieving inner success. Regardless of what you wish for, you need to create an inner fortune in order to be able to enjoy and treasure your outer successes.

A few years back, I visited a family far off in the deepest jungles of the Amazonas. This family consisted of twelve individuals and they all lived in a small hut. This hut measured about 200 square feet and it was built on posts six feet long to protect the family from the dangerous animals of the jungle. The whole family, including the young children, worked from early morning until late at night gathering food. This was both to survive, but also to put food aside if they were to suffer from flooding from the nearby river. When I arrived to the family, they welcomed me with open arms.

They invited me into their home and made me a superb dinner. It is easy to think that one would pity this family for living under such extremely harsh conditions. They were completely cut off from the rest of the world, without electricity or clean water and, most likely, without any money whatsoever. The first thing that struck me, however, was that they were all positively radiant. It was as if they were engulfed in a sparkling glow of happiness and joy. One of the boys had a book and it had helped him to learn a few words in English. During a couple of hours, we talked using gestures and body language, interspersed with a few words of English. I had a lot of questions I wanted to ask him, but there was one in particular I was especially keen on hearing his reply to.

What was the recipe, or key, for their extremely powerful happiness – a happiness completely glowing here in the middle of the rainforest? Finally, after some effort, he gave me his answer: "As we live this simple life, we don't create any other desires or temptations. We have everything we need here to be happy. We need nothing else."

As the sun set beyond the treetops, we ended our wonderful evening with a pretty unorthodox game of soccer. Everyone played, even grandma and grandpa. The game began, and I had the honor of scoring the first goal. I reached up towards the sky in a victory gesture and smiled at my teammates, who also reached up towards the sky. When we all hugged, the other team came running, just as happy. Yes, they were really happy and they also started hugging. I explained to them that the score was now 1-0 to my team, but no one seemed to understand what I was saying and it was not because we spoke different languages. Later, the other team scored a goal, and then everyone started to cheer and hug again – also those on my team. Being pretty competitive, I found this really quite odd and I made the score even clearer by carving 1-1 in the grass, but everyone just laughed. It made no difference which team scored; they all cheered just the same.

Later, it turned out that they did not grasp the concept of competing. They had no idea whatsoever what a competition was all about, and I never managed to get them to understand it either. They just wanted someone to score. It made no difference if they or someone from the other team did it.

Nevertheless, I later left this remarkable jungle family, who gave me memories and insights I will always carry with me. One insight that these wonderful individuals passed on to me was: Everyone is born empty-handed and everyone dies empty-handed, but there is something else that will always go on living through those around us. That is our love, our life force, our joy, our wisdom and our inner self. This may live for all eternity.

10
Finding your way around the brain

Sometimes the different parts of the brain stop working together and then we have a problem. In order for us to function and to feel as good as possible, the level of coordination in our brains needs to be absolutely world-class.

The brain is made up of a number of different areas, each of which has its own function, like emotions, hearing, sight, reading comprehension, balance, breathing, speech, basic movements, sensory inputs and complex movements. These, putting it simply, consist of various centers and areas of cells, all of which specialize in one or more tasks. When, for instance, you want to read a book, the center for

motor skills is first activated, allowing you to pick up the book. Then the cerebellum is activated to adjust the movement. Sensory centers are activated when you touch the book. To be able to interpret the meaning of the text, the speech center is activated, as are different memory centers. Meanwhile, the vision center is trying to interpret the letters in the book. Repetition, just like any kind of practice, makes the different centers cooperate even better.

We will probably never be able to use our brains to their full potential, but by learning how some of the brain's functions work and cooperate, we will get a better understanding of how to make ourselves feel even better.

Create habits using the cerebellum

The brain is primarily made up of three parts: the cerebrum, the cerebellum (the small brain) and the brainstem. The cerebellum helps us to undertake coordinated movements and to store taught movement patterns, like walking, running, dancing or playing tennis. Through repetition, the synapses in the brain become more effective. The cerebrum, however, is in charge and sends out orders. It then transmits these to the cerebellum, which, in turn, automates the movements through repetition.

A common method among athletes when practicing is to devote entire sessions to only practice certain movement patterns. A badminton player may, for example, find herself all alone on the court practicing lunges. When she has practiced this movement pattern for a certain amount of time, it will get stuck in her brain's muscle memory and it will thereafter be totally automatic. What she is doing is simply "over-learning" her movement pattern. Famous Swedish tennis player Björn Borg used to hit balls against his family's garage door and golfers practice the same swing hour after hour. This method of over-learning may also be used when changing habits, thought patterns and feelings.

Activate the brain's feel-good substances

When we do the things we like, we feel good. This feeling is created when the brain's reward system is activated. The brain's reward system consists of nerves and when we feel good, neurotransmitters are sent out from these nerves. They go on to stimulate receptors and other nerve cells.

We would probably not be able to feel any kind of satisfaction whatsoever without the brain's reward system. Scientists say that the reason for us having a reward system in the first place is so that we enjoy the things necessary for our survival – as individuals and as a species – like sex for procreation and food in order to not starve.

Scientists tell us that the reward system likes predictability, as this gives a sense of security and control. This, in turn, gives a sense of freedom and independence. The reward system also likes fairness and a sense of belonging.

The reward system can be your best friend or your worst enemy. As soon as you find a new pleasure, more nerves are connected in your brain and the memory of this pleasure is stored in your cerebral cortex. You could say that the reward system makes you addicted to new pleasures. If you have once activated your reward system with coffee, love, attention, exercise, good food, drugs, alcohol or whatever the case may be, then the brain will make sure that you keep having an urge for just the thing that initially activated the reward system.

We have many neurotransmitters in the brain and how these work together decides how we behave and how we feel. The following are the most common neurotransmitters:

GABA – muscle relaxant and mitigates anxiety.
Glutamate – memory and learning.
Dopamine – the body's own reward and happiness hormone. It also affects sleep, mood, concentration, learning, voluntary movements, behavior, motivation and other creative processes.
Endorphin – happiness hormone, pain reliever and digestion.
Serotonin – the purpose of this neurotransmitter is to balance out our emotions and it affects our mood, appetite, anger and so on.
Oxytocin – the body's anti-stress hormone.
Noradrenalin – excitement, being awake and stress hormone.

Of all the neurotransmitters, dopamine is the one that primarily activates the brain's reward system. It is released when we do something we enjoy, like exercising, spending time with friends, having a nice meal and laughing. Empathy, altruism and being kind also activates the reward system. Doing things we like, which are also new to us, increases the production even more. In today's society, we are constantly seeking small dopamine injections – cellphones, in particular, is a very popular "dopamine mine." If we have not checked out our cellphone for a while, then we like to turn it on to see if we have received any exciting new text messages, e-mails or if anything fun is happening on Facebook. After a small dopamine injection, we put the phone away and go on working, studying, watching a movie or whatever we were doing before. A lot of people like their phones so much that they even bring them along when they go to bed. Before falling asleep, they lie underneath their covers and read on their phones. By the way, I have a friend who likes his cellphone so much that he falls asleep with it resting on his chest.

Oxytocin is the body's anti-stress hormone and it is released through hugging, cuddling, sex and being close. Production of oxytocin is also stimulated when we talk to someone we like. That is one of the reasons why we like spending time with family, our partner or close friends. Oxytocin makes us feel calm and relaxed, and it also stimulates growth and healing. This, in other words, is an important substance that we should try to produce. Oxytocin is not only released through social and physical interactions between people – it may also be released by being close to an animal, by petting a dog or having a purring cat in our lap.

So, what about those who live very lonely lives, without anyone around them and without any pets? In these cases there are other ways of increasing the production of oxytocin. Everything giving us pleasure, joy and a nice feeling – warm baths, the sun, music or having a massage – increases the production of oxytocin. When more oxytocin is released, we tend to become friendlier. If your colleague is annoyed and in a foul mood, then you may increase his oxytocin production by speaking to him in a pleasant and soft voice or by giving him a friendly look. At the business meeting, you can use your friendly tone of voice and say hello with a warm and welcoming handshake. The better someone likes being around you, the more oxytocin he will produce, which, in turn, will make him more accommodating and cooperative. Perhaps this is something worth considering when discussing your next pay raise?

The "smart" frontal lobe talks sense with the sensitive amygdala

Brain scientists say that the frontal lobe is the smartest part of the brain. This is where our reasoning originates. Meanwhile, the amygdala is the brain's number one center for feelings. Feelings move much faster than thoughts and they also travel the same neural pathways in our brains. This is how our feelings and thoughts work together: When we see something that could be dangerous, vision impulses are sent to both the frontal lobe and the amygdala. While the frontal lobe is dealing with the potentially dangerous signals through reasoning, the amygdala immediately turns on its alarm system. This alarm system is based on previous experiences. If we have not already experienced something similar, then the signals from the amygdala are much weaker, which allows for our reasoning to put a stop to the feelings.

Personally, I have had bad experiences going to the dentist, so I get very scared every time my yearly check-up comes along. Others, who may have more pleasant experiences going to see the dentist, react much calmer.

Extremely terrifying memories lead to small signals creating a sense of panic. It is enough with just a small worrying sign for the alarm system of the amygdala to kick into full gear. For me, all it takes is the dentist turning on the drill or hearing the dreaded words: "I think I see a cavity." Here, the frontal lobe is not given the opportunity to calm me down with logical arguments saying that the dentist has a good education, a lot of experience and is very careful. I used to have to bring an extra shirt when going to the dentist, as I got completely soaked from sweating so much. Today, fortunately, things are not quite that bad.

Activating our "smart" frontal lobe reduces the worrying activities in the amygdala. The warning signals of the amygdala obviously have an important role to play as they warn us about dangerous situations, but there is also a downside. Since our prior experiences leave behind different kinds of traces, the amygdala also sends out false alarms. The sensitive amygdala will become active in response to all kinds of emotions, like fear, anxiety and grief. At the same time, the frontal lobe is trying to calm us down by creating a sense of understanding through reasonable arguments. There are many situations that may upset us or make us sad or frightened, but the better we get at stopping and reflecting on these situations, the better we will understand them. This kind of understanding makes the amygdala and the frontal lobe work together much better.

I have a very strong memory playing a game of table tennis when I was eleven. I remember playing as best as I possibly could and that I was about to win this semifinal. I was ahead by 20-9 in the deciding set and I only needed to win one more point to win the game. Then something very peculiar happened. I lost 13 points in a row and my opponent turned the game around against all odds. My dream of going on to the final was rapidly evaporating. The stands were totally packed and I sensed that the audience was in a state of shock over what had just happened. This, obviously, was my own personal experience of the situation, which was intensified by my own feelings. The question is how this nightmarish situation affected me as a young boy and if it affected the functions in my brain.

This experience affected me in such a way that for the next year, I became very nervous whenever I had a match point. I did not get all that nervous when I was ahead by something like 20-5, but if my lead was less than something like 20-9, I became terribly nervous. I remember thinking that this was really strange, because at the same time I also used to play tennis, and I never got nervous playing tennis. What was happening here was that my amygdala turned on all the bells and whistles in its alarm central, signaling fear, whenever I had a match point in a table tennis game. The sense of fear led to the following thought: “In front of full stands and a shocked audience, I end up losing with a score of 20-9 in the last and deciding set. What if it happens again?” During this year, I nevertheless managed to defeat my demons and even to win a few games of table tennis. As time went by, the amygdala became more reasonable to the sensible arguments from the frontal lobe and never set off any more false alarms.

By increasing our awareness of situations that previously frightened us, we may in the future quickly identify possible false alarms and, subsequently, get the ability to block unwelcome feelings. This is how our brains react to almost all kinds of feelings. If you were bitten by a vicious dog as a kid, chances are that your amygdala will continue to signal danger as soon as you see a dog. If you make a huge mistake at work, then this particular situation may trigger your amygdala in the future. A person who has been in a relationship with someone who turned out to be cheating may have big issues with trust in the future. The amygdala whips up its whole alarm system at the tiniest amount of anxiety or suspicion. If we do not try to understand and heal from earlier wounds, then we cannot at the same time expect that the frontal lobe will be able to convince the sensitive amygdala with its logical arguments. To simplify, you could say that when we have a lot of time to assess the signal of danger, it has enough time to reach the frontal lobe and we may steer clear. Conversely, if we do not have the time to reflect, then the signal goes straight to the amygdala, which then sounds the alarm.

The amygdala and the frontal lobe work in shifts

The sensitive amygdala and the "smart" frontal lobe need to be able to work together for you to feel good. This is because the frontal lobe gets tired after having been active for too long. The amygdala, on the other hand, may stay active for a longer period of time, since the mental activities taking place there are simpler and more automatic.

By letting these two work in shifts, you let your "smart" brain rest ahead of more important tasks requiring more mental activity. Let them relieve one another by creating a large degree of variety in your daily tasks. If you are aware of the need for saving your "smart" frontal lobe, then you will be at your absolute sharpest when you need it the most.

Think about when you feel the sharpest and try to adjust your day accordingly. Do you feel that you are the sharpest in the mornings? Do the things that require you to think the most before lunch and do the simpler things in the afternoon. Another way of saving the mental powers of your frontal lobe is to write down what you are to do during the day, week and month. This way, you do not have to waste the valuable powers of the frontal lobe by having to remember all the things you need to do.

The frontal lobe's eternal struggle with the reptilian brain

The primitive brain, also referred to as the reptilian brain, is responsible for some of the brain's more instinctive decisions, like making a few quick bucks or having a little bit too much chocolate. This is the part of the brain we need to control in order to steer clear of all kinds of temptations.

Your frontal lobe is incredibly smart and it makes it possible for you to have the most complex of thoughts. While your frontal lobe is very active, it is easy for you to shut out the kinds of distractions that tempt your reptilian brain.

When we are hungry, the reptilian brain gives us signals like: "Have that candy bar!" Or, if we are facing financial hardships, it may give us signals like: "Grab that opportunity to earn those quick bucks!" By practicing the discipline of the reptilian brain, it will be easier for us to resist various temptations. There are also simple methods for keeping our reptilian brain calm. If we eat well, then we will not be as tempted by that candy bar, and through the rational thoughts of our frontal lobe, we are less tempted by that get-rich-quick scheme.

"The lizard effect"

The "smart" frontal lobe is something that sets adult humans apart from animals. Thanks to the frontal lobe, we have the ability to assess and resist the temptations of quick rewards. This ability makes it possible for us to keep a bag of candy in order to eat it on Saturday. Thanks to our developed frontal lobe, we also have the ability to decline receiving $50 today instead of receiving $60 tomorrow.

The frontal lobes in children, on the other hand, are not as developed as those in adults. In order to understand how children react to long-term and short-term rewards, a famous experiment was undertaken that has been called the marshmallow test. A group of 5-year-olds got to sit for a few minutes looking at a marshmallow. If they could resist this very tempting marshmallow for 15 minutes, then they would get another one. A lot of them failed and instead ate it immediately. A few, though, waited the full 15 minutes before eating the marshmallow.

Years later, a follow-up study was undertaken, which showed that the kids who were able to resist the temptation to eat their marshmallow were more successful than the rest when it came to getting a good education and later having a good and well-paid job. The study concluded that children with the ability to be disciplined and resist the impulses of the reptilian brain had a great advantage later in life.

If we look at animals, we see that they work much the same as children. They simply do not have the ability to imagine the future the same way adult humans do. A lizard, for example, cannot evaluate and delay a temptation in order to get an even larger reward later. The spooky thing about us humans is that when we are stressed, we let the reasoning abilities of the frontal lobe diminish. This leads to the reptilian brain working more and more and taking greater responsibilities. When this happens, our behavior become more similar to that of a lizard. In today's stressed-out society, we suffer from this lizard effect alarmingly often.

11
Use your brain

Most scientists studying the human brain agree that it is actually constructed for being used 40,000 years ago. So, how do we use it to feel good today?

The brain is enormously powerful and it is also very complex. Without us noticing, the brain guides us in different directions when it comes to behavior, actions, thoughts and feelings. Learning a few very interesting facts about the brain makes it possible for us to use more of its vast potential.

Your brain loves to see its own reflection

One really fascinating aspect about the brain are the so-called mirror neurons. These affect us in that our brains tend to mirror events. When we see someone doing something, our brains think that we are doing the same thing. I know – it sounds weird – but please let me explain. What happens when you see someone cutting his finger? Do you flinch or do you even say "ouch"? My guess is that you feel that person's pain in one way or another. If a colleague relates to you when she recently had eye surgery, does that not make you feel somewhat uncomfortable?

Seeing or hearing the pain, joy, sorrow or enthusiasm of others transmits that same feeling over to us. Let us say that you are in a meeting with a colleague. If he starts to wave his arms around and raising his tone of voice, then it is very easy for you to start doing the same. If you are in a competitive setting, then you may sometimes have to compete against opponents who are unsportsmanlike. My guess is that this person's unsportsmanlike attitude subconsciously influences the way you act during this game.

What if you meet someone who is smiling? The mirror neurons in your brain will influence you to smile back. Your brain is acting according to what it sees. It acts in the same way as if you were the one smiling.

Brain scientists claim that there are two reasons why we have mirror neurons. First, they assist us in social interactions, helping us understand and comprehend other people's situations. They, in other words, help us to feel empathy. Second, they assist us when learning motor skills, especially when we are learning new things.

So, how are we to use these mirror neurons to feel and become even better? Let us start by looking at how we can make use of our mirror neurons to feel better. If we smile a lot, then the people we meet will smile back at us more frequently. If we have a friendly tone, so will the people we meet. If we laugh, others will laugh with us. And if we show love and compassion, love and compassion shall come to us as well. The energy we reflect will be mirrored in the people we meet. There are countless examples, so why not try and see how it works for you?

The simple fact that the brain thinks we are actually doing the same thing we see someone else doing illustrates, in my view, the importance of spending time with friends with the kind of qualities we value. Consider who you would like to mirror.

Furthermore, as discussed above, the mirror neurons also have an impact on how we learn motor skills. This means that we get better by watching others doing something. Let us say that you want to improve your golf game, then why not spend time watching others playing golf in order to get better? If you want to give better lectures, then go and listen to others giving lectures. If you want to be an even nicer person, then spend time with others who are nice. Remember that your brain mirrors everything it sees, like joy, happiness, positive thinking and having faith in the future.

How does your memory work?

The part of your brain responsible for your memory is called the hippocampus, which is divided into an automatic memory system and a system you control. Professor Eric Hanse, who is active in the field of neurophysiology at the Swedish University of Gothenburg, describes the memory process as going through three steps. First, we code a memory. Then we store it and, finally, we recall it. Memories are scattered all throughout the cerebral cortex and will be found and activated through the questions we ask. When we learn new things, the information is first sent to our short-term memory, after which some of the information is passed along to the long-term memory. For the brain to be able to send instructions to the rest of the body, and for us to be able to learn new things, the brain cells connect with one another. This is a constantly ongoing process and when the connection between the cells remains for a longer period of time, the basis for a new memory is created.

When we think back to something that happened in the past, new neural pathways are created in the brain, which then change its structure. This means that we distort our memory. So, in other words, when we reminisce about something that happened years ago, the brain tends to add and subtract things that are not really a part of this particular memory.

Fears and emotional experiences tend to linger in the long-term memory. Removing a fear from our memory often necessitates us being exposed to this fear. Some fears are so deeply rooted that it may take a long time to erase them, but it is possible to erase practically any kind of fear. We frequently think that the purpose of our memory is to store things, but its real purpose is to help us face the future.

Something that greatly affects our memory is stress. We all have a system for regulating our stress level, but this system will break down if we subject ourselves to too much stress. I am sure that you have also experienced temporarily forgetting a word, an event, a name or a place, while your friend is waiting for you to give her an answer. Your friend is waiting patiently, but for now it seems impossible for you to come up with the answer. But when your friend loses her patience and starts to talk, then you will remember.

What is happening here is that the brain gets stuck due to temporary stress and is not able to function properly until your friend starts talking and your stress level goes down. This is when you remember the answer.

The hippocampus regulates the stress level, and, because of this, it may be reduced in size by up to 15%. What this means is that you damage this part of the brain when you are stressed. Due to this, we often have a harder time finding our way around when we are stressed, in addition to simply forgetting more things. The brain uses different connections depending on whether we are in the process of solving a problem or whether we are stuck trying to solve it. This means that you need to create new connections when you are stuck trying to solve a problem. When you feel that your brain is stuck, take a short break and do something completely different for a while. Have a cup of coffee with your co-workers or call a good friend. After that, your brain will be able to solve the problem.

Your gut feeling is also based on memories, which are based on previous experiences and feelings. These are the kind of memories that can sometimes cause you to sweat, get nervous and so on. When you have to make a decision, your gut feeling always has a number of options. Ordinarily, it will pick the alternative associated with the highest amount of rewards and the least amount of penalty and discomfort. The more experience you have in a specific area, the stronger the gut feeling you will have. But if you are frightened or emotional, then your gut feeling may trick you. What this means is that it is always a good idea to avoid making important decisions in emotional situations.

Your brain is tricking you

We need to be aware of the fact that the brain is a master at filling in information that is not really there. This is due to a number of factors; one reason being that our sense of sight takes up most of the brain's attention. Sometimes we end up in situations where the brain is forced to rely on sight or one of the other senses. As sight takes up such a big part of the brain, it tends to choose sight. This could result in the brain simultaneously seeing one thing, smelling something else and hearing something different. If the brain is unable to cope with all of these sensations, it will choose to trust what it sees. What you see does not necessarily have to be absolutely true. The fact that you do not have enough time to register all the other inputs means that you do not get the whole picture. This is when the brain fills in information that is not really there.

Your brain simplifies and cheats

Your brain stores and influences everything you experience, but there is absolutely no way that you can register everything that happens. Scholars claim that your brain has mastered the art of using shortcuts, simplifying and jumping to conclusions (sometimes too quickly) in order not to overflow with sensory inputs. It is impossible for the brain to process everything that happens, so in order to keep functioning, it has to decide what to observe. These shortcuts, however, work as different kinds of traps, as they provide us with faulty information. Let us look at a few examples: You are driving your car and all of a sudden you meet a reckless driver. What do you think? Perhaps you think something like: "How can he drive like that? What an idiot!" Let us reverse the situation and imagine that you are the reckless driver. What do you think then? Maybe you think along the lines of: "Man, the sun is really strong today. Who would have thought I'd get so blinded that I couldn't even see the road?" These kinds of logical errors are extremely common. That is to say that when we do something wrong, then it has to do with the situation, and when someone else does the same thing, it is about them as people.

Another popular shortcut is that we tend to like people who remind us of ourselves. The brain is very lazy and it prefers to be able to recognize things. Meeting people who are different from ourselves means that the brain has to work a little bit harder. Sometimes the brain is not able to put in the time and effort to give this person a fair chance, which leads to us jumping to conclusions too quickly or simply withdrawing.

I don't know about you, but isn't your dog or cat just a little bit cuter than all the others? And, surely, isn't that toolshed you built or that plant you just planted a little bit nicer than everyone else's? This is completely normal, as we tend to think that things are particularly nice, smart, effective, brilliant or beautiful when we have been involved.

Another logical error we often encounter is when we subconsciously put too much stock in our own abilities. Experiments show that when we are 100% sure, we are actually wrong in 20% of all cases.

Imagine how you would react if your husband comes home and tells you that he has found a used car he thinks you should buy. He says that it is cool, practical, well-maintained and scratched. If he instead were to say that the car is scratched, well-maintained, practical and cool, do you think that you would react differently? The fact that our perception of what we hear is influenced by what we hear first would probably lead you to react completely differently even though each sentence contains the exact same words. Starting out a sentence with the word cool, instead of scratched, will improve your chances of the receiver experiencing the purchase more positively.

The brain's greatest love

Have you considered why your favorite dish is not as good if you eat it day after day? It is because the brain loves to be stimulated through variety. It simply reacts to contrasts and, according to brain researcher Katarina Gospic, the most important task of the brain is to distinguish contrasts. There is a structure in the brain called the orbitofrontal cortex, which updates and decides what, at the moment, is a reward. The more you do something you like, the less the orbitofrontal cortex will code this particular thing as a reward.

Conversely, this structure is more than willing to code new things as being rewards. If you eat chocolate for four days straight, then you will probably enjoy it the most the first day. This is also the reason why the first piece of chocolate in the box is often the most satisfying. The same goes for alcohol.

All kinds of contrasts are a break from the blindness of everyday life. Let us imagine that you are looking for a new job. You go to three interviews, where all three people interviewing you are rude and unpleasant. If the person at the fourth company is nice and pleasant, then how will you react and would you react the same way if everyone at the first three companies were just as nice? This is kind of similar to how we work when trying to achieve a goal. The more we fail at reaching a goal, the stronger the reward signals will be when we finally succeed. If you are watching TV and all you see are pretty lousy shows, then your experience will become even stronger if you switch over to something that is actually OK.

The brain's eternal love for contrasts is based on our tendency to getting used to rewards. When you do something often, the reward signals will decrease. Nevertheless, there are effective ways of tricking the brain. All kinds of variety fulfill the brain's need for contrasts. The contrast between the big city and the wilderness. The contrast between staying at home at night and going out to meet friends. Varied kinds of exercise – spinning one day, dancing the next day followed by strength training the third. Having variety at work or varying travel destinations, adventures, treats, forms of entertainment, friends, walks, coffee shops, meals and interests.

Another way of tricking the brain to get the reward signals flowing is to spice up your activities, like walking or travelling with new friends, lighting even more candles on your cozy nights staying in or working out with some kind of coach.

The experience is governed by your expectations

In order for us to function optimally, our neurotransmitters need to be in balance with one another. Some situations may upset this balance, which could result in chaos. When we have just fallen in love, our levels of dopamine and noradrenaline increase, while the serotonin level decreases. This may cause us to forget about space and time, and the only thing that matters to us is to be with the person we love. We may have a hard time concentrating and in some cases it may even be hard to work, as our thoughts and feelings are all focused on the euphoric sensation of being in love. The brain always has an expectation as to how something should be, and when these kinds of emotions arise, the brain automatically evaluates them to see if they are better or worse than expected. When it is better than expected, the balance between the neurotransmitters is upset. The feeling of just having fallen in love moves on to the next phase when it is no longer possible to surpass expectations.

Scientists say that new love between people usually lasts for about 18 months. Humans are fortunate – love between animals is said to be much shorter. Elephants, for instance, are in love for about three months, dogs for two and birds are only in love for three to four days.

Every brain is unique and we react differently to different things. Some people get an enormous sense of satisfaction when eating chocolate, whereas others get it by running a marathon. An interesting aspect about the reactions in our reward system is that we can learn to replace one source of pleasure with another. It is possible, if we so wish, to learn how to replace the pleasure of chocolate with working out at the gym for 30 minutes, or we may replace the chocolate bar with a nice dinner. But in order for us to enjoy working out, instead of eating chocolate, we need to create the feeling of longing to work out. When we look forward to working out, we have created an expectation and this is when we experience pleasure. However, we also need to make sure that our expectations are realistic in order not to trick ourselves. The fact that we like quick rewards may sometimes lead to us convincing ourselves that some things are easier or better than they really are. Hence, we trick ourselves and the reward system's signals are considerably weaker than if our expectations were more

realistic. What this means is that your experiences are ruled by your expectations. Most likely, you sometimes feel that an experience does not live up to your expectations, and instead of the reward system creating a nice feeling, you get disappointed.

I remember being in my upper teens when I used to go out and have fun with my friends. Every weekend was a blast, whereas holidays such as New Year's or Midsummer were just so-so. We were never able to figure out why, but the fact of the matter was that we simply had unrealistic expectations about these special nights. In reality, we had just as fun as always, but we often came to see these particular holidays as failures.

It is the same at work. If you expect the boss to give you a raise of $200 a month, but you only receive $150, then the reaction of the reward system will be weaker. If, on the other hand, you get a raise of $250, then your reaction will be stronger. If you expect to finish a task in four hours, but it takes you seven, then the reaction from the reward system will be weaker. If you finish in three hours, then your reaction will be stronger. The same is true if you expect to easily win a game of soccer, but you only win it by 1-0 instead of 7-0.

Have you ever imagined that your upcoming vacation will be simply wonderful and you imagine that you will relax and do all the things you never have the time for otherwise? You had all of these expectations about everything you and your family were going to do and experience. But, all of a sudden, your vacation is over and it was not nearly as fantastic as you had expected. Expecting great things to happen in the future is a good thing, but building up your expectations to unrealistic proportions will weaken your reward signals. Putting it simply – your expectations decide how strongly you experience things.

This definitely does not mean that we should cease to expect the best in life. Having high expectations about yourself and your future, as we have seen above, has a very positive effect on the actual outcome. It is about creating our own balance, where we may in some cases lessen our expectations in order to let the reward system give us stronger signals. This could, for instance, be done in situations you encounter when you travel. Imagine it being 3 p.m. and you have had a perfect day with your friends. Now try to think along the lines of: "We have experienced so many great things today, so everything that happens from now on is simply a bonus." I promise you that your experience of the rest of the day will be much stronger.

12
Create a fit and rejuvenated brain

Your brain is constantly evolving. Your brain today will not be the same tomorrow. The crucial factor for whether your brain gets stronger or weaker is what you fill it with.

Your feelings are ruled by your brain, and the fact that the brain is constantly flexible and able to evolve makes it possible for everyone to create their own brain. You have a tremendous ability to influence the way your brain evolves. Scholars claim that we can maintain a fit brain throughout our whole lives. Sure, our memory gets worse and we may tend to forget things as we get older, but the brain does not necessarily have to deteriorate. Photographing the activity in the brain, we usually see more light parts the younger we are. The more light parts, the healthier the brain. Despite the fact that the brain gets more and more dark parts the older we get, there is actually a lot we can do to counteract this.

The structures in the brain are constantly evolving. They change when we do things like reading, fantasizing or thinking. Just as with everything else in life, we need to constantly look after and nurture the brain, whilst constantly giving it the right kind of nourishment. When we take care of the brain, we help our brain cells to stay connected with one another, which is very important for how we feel mentally as well as physically. We often have a much better idea as to how to take care of our body to ensure that it feels OK. We know that we can achieve a fit body, as well as rejuvenating it, through things like exercise and having a good diet. But how do we achieve a fit and rejuvenated brain? What kinds of nourishments do you need to light up that brain of yours?

Mental exercise

It becomes noticeable in our faces and our bodies when we get older. Even though it is not possible to see, the brain gets older in just the same way. We keep our muscles active through physical activities, and we keep our brains active through mental activities. We, in other words, keep our brains active by using them. There are many things you can do to give your brain an effective workout: memory training, sudoko, crossword puzzles or learning new things. You increase the number of receptors, which capture and then send signals along, when you exercise your brain. Carl-Gerhard Gottfries, MD and professor emeritus in clinical neuroscience, claims that the more receptors you have, the better brain functions like memory or speech will become.

Physical exercise

Examining older individuals who have not had a regular exercise regimen, it is noticeable that their brains get darker and darker. Looking at older individuals who, on the contrary, have been more careful to exercise regularly, you see about the same amount of light parts as in young people. You could say that the body has its own pharmacy and that the absolute best way to activate this pharmacy is to keep moving your body. We know that this is beneficial to the heart, but it is just as important for the brain. When we are out having a run, for instance, the connections in our brains improve and we think more clearly. Maybe that is why a lot of people exercise before important meetings – to get that extra edge. When we are running, broken connections in the brain are fixed, and that is why running and other kinds of physical exercise calm us down when we are stressed. Exercise improves our mood and strengthens our defenses against depressions. Exercise works as the brain's cure, while also increasing our overall well-being.

According to many brain scientists, our brains start to deteriorate in our 30s and the part that starts to go first is the "smart" frontal lobe. This, however, does not have to be a problem as it is possible to rejuvenate the brain through regular exercise.

Stimulate your brain

The more you already know, the easier it becomes for you to learn even more. What this means is that your brain will become even smarter tomorrow if you learn something new today. Scientists say that the brain is one great network and that everything we remember is stored in the shape of connections/synapses between the brain cells. The more you use it and the more you store things, the better it works. When you use the brain, connections/synapses are created, which then work together. The network in the brain consists of a hundred billion brain cells, and each and every one of these is connected with thousands of other cells. New connections are formed when we learn new things.

When someone becomes inactive and therefore does not provide the brain with the stimuli it needs, the brain starts to regress. Older people sometimes find themselves in a situation where they are lonely and isolated from the outside world. This has an extremely negative effect on the brain. The brain needs to be constantly stimulated and this is achieved, among other things, when we spend time with others. Primarily, the brain is stimulated when we are curious and when we have fun. Many scientists say that older people should play more. In Finland, they have built a kindergarten for old people where they can play around and have a really good time. This has vastly stimulated the brains of the participants.

A study released in 2008 has shown that the Internet also has a very positive effect on the brain. The brain evolves rapidly for someone learning to use the

Internet. After having been online for a week, this study showed a higher level of activity in the brain.

It has also been argued that the brain gets stimulated when we do things for others, like getting involved in charities and non-profit organizations, or when we spend time with children or grandchildren. American psychiatrist Gene D. Cohen concluded in a study that older people who had developed an interest in art became healthier and more independent. Music and other forms of cultural expressions, according to many scholars, also have a positive effect on the brain. The cultural stimuli raise our heart rate and when we listen to music, we create mental images and we fantasize. Something that greatly stimulates the brain is when both its cerebral hemispheres are activated at the same time. This has a great impact on the synapses in the brain. It is possible for you to create this effect by, for example, dancing. This simultaneously activates both the speech center as well as the center for movement.

It is not necessary to change a lot of things in order to stimulate the brain. It is sufficient to have a hobby, read, write or getting some fresh air to pick up different scents. Scientists say that joy and growth are basic human needs. When we fulfill these needs, we become less vulnerable to the so-called free radicals. These have a negative effect on the brain and make us grow old faster.

Exercise your brain into thinking positive thoughts

Negative thoughts harm your brain. Nils Simonson, former surgeon and author of a number of books on how the brain works, says that having a positive outlook has many benefits for your brain. He says that optimists on average live almost eight years longer than pessimists. There are many indications that we can think ourselves ill or healthy.

Having a sense of meaning

When we do not fulfill our need to have meaning, we create an inner stress. This, in turn, has many negative effects on the brain.

How stress affects you

Consciously and subconsciously, your brain processes all the information it receives. Every day, your brain processes everything from thousands of positive and negative events to things like challenges, strains and discomforts. When you are stressed, the brain sends out impulses through the body's stress system, which is made up of nerves and hormones. In order to assist the body in dealing with stress, impulses are sent out and this initiates different reactions throughout the body.

When we feel stressed, the body is subconsciously beginning to prepare itself for fight or flight, which is something passed on to us from our distant ancestors. This stress function is crucial for us to be able to stay alive. The stress function used to take a completely different form earlier in our history. Back then, stress was activated so that we would be able to physically survive life-threatening situations on the savannah. Today, our stress function is activated when we fall behind at work, when the car breaks down and when we are late. Perhaps this was not its original purpose.

So, what happens in the body when we feel stressed? Former surgeon Nils Simonson says that negative stress activates the adrenal glands' production of cortisol. This hormone shrinks the hippocampus in the brain and it is precisely this area that transforms short-term memories into long-term ones. He writes that the hippocampus works as some sort of a librarian sorting through and categorizing our memories in the cerebral cortex when we sleep. Someone suffering from stress and sleep deprivation risks having his memories sorted incorrectly.

The adrenal glands not only produce cortisol when we experience stress, they also produce the stress hormones adrenaline and noradrenaline. When the stress function is activated, neural impulses are sent out to the brain along the spinal cord to the body's various organs, which, in turn, often react with pain. Short-term stress is positive and this kind of stress is also beneficial to the immune system. The cortisol produced during stress has anti-inflammatory properties that protect us from illnesses or feeling tired. This is why we may temporarily feel well again when working out or being stressed. This could also explain why so many get sick during their vacations, as we then slow down and decrease the level of stress in our everyday lives.

Positive stress sharpens your senses and increases your performance. This could manifest itself when you are under time pressure or when you find yourself in an emergency, but also when you work out. As long as this kind of stress does not last for too long or happens too frequently, it may be beneficial to you.

The brain truly is a champion when it comes to keeping a number of different processes going on at the same time, like handling our tasks at work, planning for the future, thinking about what we want to do when we get off work, what to get at the grocery store or what to have for lunch, in addition to a great number of subconscious processes like observations and automatic thoughts. What happens in the brain when you experience positive stress is that the brain automatically shuts down unnecessary processes. This means that you can focus 100% on one single task. This could be something like a deadline at work or an athletic performance.

We also have negative stress and that does not only manifest itself when you have a lot to do. It can also accumulate through boredom or anxiety. A very common reason for experiencing stress is not being stimulated enough. Many people today work solely to make money and it is not uncommon that this leads to stress. Carl-Gerhard Gottfries claims that persistent and chronic stress makes the brain grow old faster. Stress may have a multitude of harmful effects on our health. Among other things, it is clear that stress quite frequently leads to depression. Some American studies from 2010 also conclude that depression almost doubles the risk of developing dementia.

Three steps to cope with stress

The first step is learning how to identify stress. Exactly how stress manifests itself varies greatly from individual to individual. Some get headaches, their bodies hurt, they sweat or have difficulties sleeping. Others may feel extremely tired or experience fatigue.

The second step is to find out the reason for you being stressed. Do certain situations create inner stress or is it something in your own behavior?

The third step is about drawing up a plan on how to avoid stress in the future and finding methods for dealing with stress when it arises.

It is easy to simply blame stress on having a lot to do at work, or in our lives in general, but the fact of the matter is that we always have the option of changing our situation. Let us say that you have identified stress as a cause for your deteriorating health, and that you have also come to the realization that your job is the crucial factor for why you are stressed. In that case, you really need to consider whether or not staying at your current job is actually worth it. Maybe you need to list the pros and cons of taking a new job. The pros could be something like less stress and more leisure time, while the cons could be things like a smaller salary and less status. Ask yourself how your life would be affected if you experienced less stress at work and had more time off. I guess it would mean improved health and more time to do the things you really like: for instance, spending time with your family and friends or putting aside more time towards your hobbies.

When stress takes over our lives, we tend to do away with the fun and pleasurable things that make us feel really good. We simply feel that we have to prioritize in order to have the time to do everything we need to do. But the fact of the matter is that this is precisely when the brain and the body need to experience pleasure and having fun the most.

Scientists say that the stress level decreases when we do things like playing, when we have a good time and after a workout. Another good cure for stress is to relax – things like yoga, watching a movie, taking a walk in nature, reading a book and exercising. Some people cure stress by having calming thoughts. When they are attacked by stress, they shift their thoughts to a setting, phase or place in life they love. And this is how they are able to decrease their stress level.

If you have a stressful job you also happen to like, then you can regulate the stress level by taking short breaks. Organizing how you spend your time gives you a clear structure when it comes to your everyday life, and this structure makes it possible for a lot of people to reduce the feeling of being stressed. Get good at delegating and learn to sometimes surrender control. Something else that may help you to reduce your stress level is to stop putting off things that make you feel uncomfortable.

Also practice something as tricky as being able to say no. Have the courage to say no when your boss asks you to work overtime, have the courage to say no to some dinner parties and even have the courage to sometimes say no when people ask you for help. Simply have the courage to say no to things you really do not want to do. The art of saying no is an exceedingly effective method for lowering the level of stress.

Studies show that we become less resilient towards stress the older we get. This does not necessarily have to be a problem, because as long as we are aware of this, we may try to adapt our daily lives to this fact.

People with a high threshold for stress are often good at only thinking of one thing at a time. Some people may live a very stressful life, but have an attitude that results in them not feeling stressed. Greek philosopher Epictetus once said: "Men are disturbed, not by things, but by the principles and notions which they form concerning things." It is important to understand that it is hardly ever the situations or the problems themselves creating stress, but rather how we perceive them. Stress, in other words, is created by our interpretation and perception of what happens around us. Consider, for example, heads of states, executives in large companies, doctors or others who work under extremely stressful and difficult circumstances all around the world. We may also turn our gaze towards our own lives and consider the general differences between the stress hormones of men and women. As the man comes home to his family after a long day at work, his stress hormones decrease, whereas they tend to increase for the woman when she comes home.

If you experience stress in your everyday life or at work, you may consider whether this stems from having unreasonably high demands on yourself, or if you perhaps tend to blame yourself when things go wrong.

Sleep

Scientists claim that when we sleep, the brain primarily does three things: recovering, rebuilding and repairing. Not sleeping enough makes it harder for us to use our "smart" frontal lobe. Instead, the reptile brain takes over more, and we risk experiencing the "lizard effect" (see chapter 10).

Diet

Living a healthy life is important to both brain and body. What you eat are the building blocks of your body and your brain, which means that the better food you eat, the better your body and brain will function.

Challenge the brain

It sure is nice when we are within the safe confines of life, but this is not good for our brains. The synapses of the brain need to be connected with one another and the brain reacts to contrasts. When we do new, fun and exciting things, we strengthen the brain's network of connections. When we exercise the brain, new vessels and cells are created. Learning new things, like a new language, makes the brain more powerful. If we stop learning new things and only keep on following our own footsteps, then the synapses start to go out one by one until our brains get completely dark, says Rolf Ekman, professor emeritus in neural chemistry at University of Gothenburg in Sweden.

Meditate yourself young

Meditation also creates more connections in the brain, whereas the number of current signals decreases. This gives us a chance to take a break from all of our thoughts. Meditation also affects our ability to feel empathy.

Some time ago, a study was carried out on a number of monks who devoted a great deal of time to meditation. When these monks were in their 50s, they had the mental capacities of someone in their 20s.

Brain scientists say that a good principle for taking care of your brain is to consider that everything that is good for your skin is good for your brain – for instance, a nutritious diet, vitamins, exercise and refraining from smoking.

13
Reach your mind's full potential

You have over 40,000 thoughts every day. Every thought passing through your brain may influence your emotional state of mind. Everyone carries enormous powers within themselves, but only very few let these powers flow freely. When you reach the full potential of your mind, you are able to release all of your inner life force.

The enormous power we carry within ourselves is blocked by our own thoughts, our past, our fears, our lack of self-confidence, our habits, how the outside world influences us, stress and worrying about the future.

Surely you have had days when everything simply went according to plan. On this particular day, there were no problems or worries whatsoever and you felt that you had a wonderful flow in everything you did. My guess is that you have also experienced days that were the complete opposite, where most things felt as if they worked against you. Is it just chance that some days you have this wonderful sense of flow whereas other days are just filled with trouble and strife?

Some days, you end up facing more problems than on other days, but the days where you feel that life is just moving along smoothly are your own creations. During your bad days, you may see a problem as incredibly annoying, while that same problem is solved with great ease during your days of great flow. Often, you end up solving the problem without even reflecting over it. Consider what you need for your days to have this nice flow, where everything goes your way.

For many people, these days of flow come about when the mind reaches its full potential, but the question is what we can do to reach our mind's full potential each and every day.

Focus on one thought at the time

The reason why it is so hard for us to reach our mind's full potential is because we allow our brains to run around in many different directions at the same time. You could say that your brain is like a floodlight and that there is a great flow of thoughts in the light emanating from the floodlight. More than 40,000 thoughts flow through your brain each day and most of these are the same thoughts you had already yesterday. The question is whether it is really necessary to repeat such a large part of our thoughts. The brain becomes significantly sharper if we can transform the light from being a floodlight into a razor-sharp laser beam. We all know that a laser beam, contrary to floodlights, can cut through most things in an incredibly effective manner. In the same way, our brains become much more effective if we learn to focus on one thought at a time. Our ability to concentrate and our sense of perception will be dramatically sharpened. Our creativity increases, our judgment gets sharper and we are able to think more quickly. Practice focusing on one thought, feeling and task at a time. You can apply this thought pattern to most things in life, like spending time with your family, relaxing or doing the things you do in your spare time.

When you learn to focus on one single thought or feeling at a time, the effect of everything you do will be significantly stronger. The experience will be more powerful and the sense of happiness and joy is increased. Likewise, how you experience a situation will become stronger the more attentive you are. The more you try to create your laser beam, the better you will get at doing just this.

In order for you to be able to produce that laser beam of yours, it is often sufficient to gather your thoughts towards the upcoming performance or task. When you allow your brain to direct all of its focus on one task, thought or feeling at a time, your mind will be much more powerful. When you want that little bit of extra from yourself, remind yourself to only concentrate on what you are doing at this very moment. Practice shutting out all other thoughts and feelings.

Live a healthy life

Try finding your own balance in life. The balance between a good diet, good exercise and the right amount of sleep, but also between family, friends, social activities, relaxation, work and hobbies. If you are often sick or if you frequently feel tired, find out why. Probably, you only need to make a few adjustments in how you live, eat and sleep. It could be that it only takes some tiny adjustments for you to once again be able to find that right balance.

Frequently, the necessary adjustments are obvious, but there are times when the necessary adjustments are harder to identify. We may, for instance, feel that we get enough sleep, but perhaps we do not get enough hours of deep sleep. Or, it could be that we feel that we drink enough water, but that we miss having a glass of water when we get up in the morning. We sweat at night and drinking a glass of water as soon as we wake up is a good way to quickly rehydrate.

If you feel that you completely lack energy, do something about it. Do something about it already today. Tomorrow, it could be too late.

Deal with your past

Many years ago, I would sometimes sweep the dust under the rug, just to be able to clean faster. It looked nice at the moment, but the problem was that the dust remained and would sooner or later reappear. We work the same way when we deal with our feelings. If we sweep uncomfortable situations under the rug, or if we ignore our feelings, then they will eventually resurface anyway and then more powerful than if we had dealt with them earlier. Anxiety and dwelling on things tends to suck the life out of people. The better you clean out your past, the less time you have to worry and dwell on things.

When you are bogged down by difficult feelings from your past, you tend to get constantly reminded of these unpleasant situations. You may also end up in situations where you project the difficult feelings of others onto yourself. A friend may face a problem you have also experienced, or you may be watching a sad movie, and these things make you project their feelings onto yourself. If you sort out possible difficulties from your past, you will avoid having to face disruptive situations later in life – situations that may turn out to be much more complicated.

When you clean your home and get rid of old stuff you no longer need, you create space for new things that are more useful and enjoyable today. When you clean up in your past and get rid of unwelcome thoughts and feelings, you create room for new, welcome thoughts and feelings.

Self-esteem

A strong sense of self-esteem makes us see our own value. When we do, we come to understand that we are worth nothing but the best in life. This knowledge guides our decisions and behavior towards the best.

Someone with a great sense of self-esteem has more courage to be herself. The more courageous you are about exploring your true self, the more you increase your chances of finding inner harmony. When you move outside of your true self, it becomes harder for you to achieve harmony and security. This is not all that strange, because when you try to be someone else than who you really are, you adopt a role that you are probably not 100% comfortable with.

Stop procrastinating doing things that are uncomfortable

Have you ever thought along these lines before? "I'll make that uncomfortable phone call tomorrow instead. I'll wait until next week to solve this problem." Why is it so incredibly easy for us to put off doing the things we are uncomfortable with? The risk associated with this kind of behavior is that this feeling of discomfort will only get stronger with each passing day. If we deal with problems as soon as they arise, then they will not have time to grow, and often we do not even have the time to reflect on the uncomfortable feeling surrounding this problem. Putting off the problem until tomorrow increases the risk of the power of habit taking over and we continue to put off dealing with the problem. The longer the time that passes, the more time we have to twist and turn this problem around, and eventually we see a lot of potential dangers arising from it. Sometimes it is a good idea to twist and turn a problem around, but when it comes to everyday problems, it is almost always better to deal with them as soon as they arise. Apart from the problem of disrupting your inner harmony, there is always a risk that new problems arise, which, in turn, will require your attention.

Do not let *anyone* disrupt your mood

How many times have we not let someone else affect our mood? The crazy driver, the rude sales clerk, the pushy telemarketer or the negative colleague? We will never be able to influence how others behave. The only thing we can control is how we let ourselves be influenced by their behavior. The rude sales clerk may be a complete idiot, but he does not get to decide how you react to this fact. You have the power over your own feelings.

It is very easy to get annoyed by how others behave, but if we learn to understand the underlying reasons, it becomes easier for us to cope with the behavior of others. The crazy driver, honking his horn incessantly, may be on his way to the hospital with his pregnant wife. The rude sales clerk may be experiencing deep grief, the pushy telemarketer may simply be insecure and your negative colleague may just have found out that she has a serious illness. If we remind ourselves that everyone has different backgrounds and live different lives, it becomes easier for us to overlook the bad days of those around us.

Do not let *anything* disrupt your mood

Are you one of those people who are affected by bad weather or, perhaps, by the darkness of winter? Why is that?

Having grown up in and lived most of my life in Sweden, I know all too well that winter may feel very long and dark, and I know just how wonderful it feels when spring finally arrives. The dark period of winter, however, may be just as lovely. We often experience summer as simply wonderful, as we have learned to enjoy all of its benefits, like being able to be outdoors as much as we like, sunbathing and having barbeques and picnics. In much the same way, it is possible for us to learn how to enjoy winter. This beautiful season has a lot going for it. For example, it may be much cozier watching a movie or reading a book when it is dark outside.

We sleep better when it is a little bit cooler and darker. The air is crisper and the cold temperature kills germs. A picnic in the winter, drinking a cup of hot chocolate, may be absolutely delightful.

On nice winter days, you may go skiing or ice-skating. Just imagine coming home after a really chilly day and sitting in front of the fireplace or having a nice bath. Or imagine coming home for a candlelit dinner, while you can hear the rain pouring down outside. Also consider how much easier it is to sit inside working when the weather is bad. Being locked up in an office or in a factory during a beautiful summer day is not all that fun.

During summer, we do not usually have the need to remind ourselves of the advantages of this season, but in the winter, when everything feels dark and cold, we need to remind ourselves more frequently about the benefits of this particular season. During winter, there is a significant risk that we tend to feel tired and experience fatigue. During these times, it is easy for us to take the path of least resistance and all of a sudden do less of the things that normally give us energy, like exercise, meeting friends or taking walks. During this period, we need to put more of an effort into manufacturing energy and a joy for living. We need to consider which joys and energy-boosting activities we should fill our lives with. If we succeed in doing this, while at the same time reminding ourselves of the benefits of winter, then our feelings about this period will significantly improve.

Contemplation and reflection

We need to stop what we are doing, so that we can check and regulate our inner thermostat. Life is spinning around at an incredible speed and we often tend to give ourselves not nearly enough time for contemplation and reflection. We need to regularly stop and take our temperature: "How do I feel? Why do I feel a certain way? Why do I tend to get upset in certain situations? What do I need to feel good at this moment?" When you reflect, you become better suited to face possible problems in the future.

Become the best version of you

Think about what the best version of you looks like, and then set up targets for you to be able to live up to that picture. Be careful not to compare yourself with others. You do not want to be someone else's idea of a best version. You want to be your own best version, based on your own characteristics and dreams.

Separate work and leisure

You dedicate about a third of your life to working. How much of your life do you dedicate to enjoying yourself and having fun? Work is an important part of life, but if we spend eight hours a day working, shouldn't we then stop thinking about work when we are finally free?

Some people take their work home out of pure habit. They are "only" answering a few e-mails or "only" preparing for tomorrow. Others are so busy at work that they simply feel that they have to work, even when they are off work. Ask yourself what really is the most important: your work or your family? Is it more important that your boss says that you have done a great job, or that your children tell you that you are the greatest dad in the world? Is it more important that your bank account is growing, or that you are present in the moment and get to experience your children growing up? Regardless of how much you have to do at work, you will perform better at work if you shut it out when you come home. You will experience having more energy, inspiration and power to perform the things you want to at work. In today's society, we work half of our waking hours, which is more than enough. Practice being off work when you are off work. We need to learn how to separate work from leisure and to have the courage to shut out work in order to do the things that are truly valuable to us.

Find your own tools for your feelings

As you already know, we are all different, and we all need to become experts at handling and understanding our own feelings, which may sometimes obstruct the full potential of our minds. Consider which tools and keys you need to reach the full potential of your mind as often as possible.

I was three years old when I started using my favorite expression: "good and happy." I sometimes used this phrase when I thought that someone in the family was not good or happy, but it came to be really important to me when going to bed. I needed to say "good and happy" to the whole family before I could fall asleep, and I also needed some kind of confirmation that everyone was indeed feeling good and happy. If I had a hard time falling asleep, it was usually due to the fact that I had forgotten to utter these words. When everyone else had fallen asleep, I could lie awake for hours, but as soon as I realized that I had forgotten to say the thing that was so important to me, I would call out from my bed, at the top of my lungs: "goooood and haaappy!" They were all kind and loving in my family, so from all of the bedrooms you could hear a muted and sleepy: "Yes, good and happy." After that, I was able to go to sleep. As a kid, I had no idea why this was so tremendously important to me, but somehow my mind became calm when I felt that everyone was good and happy.

A pause for your brain

Consider when you get your best ideas, have your most valuable thoughts and come to your most innovative insights. Some get them during vacation, others while driving, swimming, taking a walk or listening to music. Some ideas come to us when we sleep. In our dreams, we are free and this is when miracles can happen. Some great things are created in our dreams. Things that are actually too big and too complicated for our brains to handle when we are awake. When we are awake, we have too many thoughts and processes going through our head, blocking the brain.

For most of us, the best ideas and insights come to us when we pause. When we relax and shut out all of the everyday tasks, the brain gets a break and this is when there is room for new thoughts and perspectives. So, how are we then to reach the full potential of our minds in the middle of a workday? It is not really an option saying to the boss: "Hey, let's go have a bubble bath and work on some new ideas." But we can use the ancient method of The Heart of the Rose on a daily basis. Shut down all of the processes in your brain to only focus on one single thought. This may be very hard, so start taking mini breaks only a minute or two long to then increase the time to up to 15 minutes (see chapter 20).

Just as your body needs to recover after exercising, you also need to let your brain rest after strenuous work. By taking a short break for your brain, you once again open up the walls surrounding your brain and all of a sudden you have created a space for new energy and new ideas.

If a very close friend gave you the world's most beautiful flower, how would you like to take care of it? My guess is that you would first and foremost put it in a very nice spot in your home. You would water it and you would most likely remove dry leaves. Maybe, you would even speak to the flower to make it feel as good as possible. Your mind works exactly the same way as this beautiful flower. If you do not look after it, weeds will start to grow and, one day, your flower will wither and die. Look after and take care of your mind as if it were the most beautiful flower in the world.

14
Take the temperature on your inner self

Sometimes we need to take the temperature on our present mood. We need to learn how to read our internal thermostat.

I don't know about you, but when I feel good I have a sense that I can fix everything. I give more of myself to those around me, I make the best decisions and I get significantly more out of life. If, on the other hand, I have experienced something tragic, then that will create obstacles inside of me. I see problems and I am more prone to noticing difficulties than opportunities. The decisions I make are not as good, as they are based on false assumptions. When I feel good, more doors are opened just because I am willing to enter them. When I enter these doors, even more opportunities are created.

If you can choose how good you want to feel on a scale from one to ten, what would you choose? We often have social goals, work-related goals, goals for exercising as well as goals regarding our standard of living. Even though not everyone is completely structured when it comes to working towards their goals, we often have goals on a number of different levels. Often, however, we miss the most important goal by far – how good we want to feel. Maybe you believe that it is not necessary; it is implied that we all want to feel as good as possible, as often as possible.

Feeling good requires some commitment from us. There are a lot of things that need to work for us to feel good. One method of having a goal approach for feeling good is using a scale from one to ten. One signifies feeling really down, while ten signifies happiness and euphoria. Instinctively, we may think that our mood should always be a ten. Unfortunately, however, we tend to get used to things. This could over time lead to us ceasing to appreciate a mood that is always "maxed out." Let us say that a level five, or even seven, is the optimal one for our normal mood level. This gives us less room for valleys and more opportunities for peaks.

When you know which level you want to reach for your normal state of mind, ask yourself what your life should be like for this level to be realistic. A number of different factors may influence this goal, things like your family, work, diet, friends, spending time alone and, first and foremost, the balance between all of these factors. Also consider when you feel your absolute best. Is it when you have a sense of harmony, when you are super happy, when you have that comfortable sense of safety, when you feel free like a bird or when you feel that you are filled up to the brim with energy? I am certain that you already know what makes you feel exceedingly good and what gives you nice and great feelings. But the advantage of reflecting on this is that it will automatically put you in even more situations that make you feel good.

When you consider how you want to feel at your normal level, you create a state of consciousness that also makes you notice the days you fall below your desired mood level. Your inner thermostat will also help you when assessing different life situations. If, for instance, you are considering attending a social event you do not care for together with a colleague, then it becomes easier for you to assess whether or not it is really worth your while going. Perhaps your line of reasoning is that your mood level will fall to level two, but at the same time you take into account that it may be good for you to subject yourself to this particular situation. Maybe you believe that it will feel good afterwards. Well, then maybe it is worth your while going after all.

When we are tired or feel uninspired, we are often way too quick to accept that this day will therefore be a bad day. There is obviously no need for us to do this. Being tired, lacking inspiration or having a bad morning does not automatically result in a bad day. A somewhat magical method for raising a not-so-good mood is to simply laugh. If you can't laugh because you don't feel happy, then you can laugh to become happy. Let me explain what happens when you laugh. When you laugh, you stimulate your whole body. Your internal organs are nicely stimulated and your laugh initiates a number of pleasant processes in your body. Among other things, endorphins are released. These are the body's own happiness hormones.

Last summer, I was lying on the beach reading a book. About ten feet away is a couple, sitting in their separate deckchair. They seem to be on vacation, but neither one of them looks very happy. Without having been given a choice in the matter, I hear them discussing how disgusting the sand is, that the sun is way too hot and that motorboats really ought to be banned. The man is complaining about his job and the woman is stressed about having to go to the grocery store later on. They really do not seem happy at all. A bit further away, their five-year-old daughter is playing in the water. I cannot help getting carried away by her wonderful laughter. Her laugh is really loud and she is laughing constantly. Sitting in her inflatable bathing ring, she all of a sudden lifts her eyes towards the sky and, in a marvelous moment of happiness, exclaims: "Mom, mom, mom – this is my best day ever!" She then continues laughing.

A few years ago, I could not help hearing a few children in a sandbox positively roaring with laughter. The rain that was pouring down on them did not seem to matter one bit. One of them was sitting while the others were lying there all covered in mud and filth. And they simply could not stop laughing. Their wonderful laughter was so captivating that I could not help myself from asking if I could join them. And I could! Of course, I wanted to know what was so amazingly funny, so I asked them why they were laughing so hard. Their answer was: "Laughing is so much fun."

Laughing is terrific for our well-being. One could say that laughter works as sort of an inner massage, a massage for the soul. Studies show that children on average laugh and smile more than 300 times per day, whereas adults only do it 15 times per day.

As you already know, there are countless things that could bring our mood down. Sometimes we worry about work or the future or our children, but sometimes our mood goes down because we actually miss something in life. A few years ago, I was talking to an 82-year-old lady. She told me that she felt a great sense of emptiness and that she was feeling very lonely. After having talked for a while, she told me that she needed something to look forward to. I asked her why she didn't and then she simply said: "Well, this might seem a bit odd, but I think I'm just going to book a trip to Rome. I've always wanted to go there." This was her key for raising her mood level. Instead of focusing on feeling lonely, she had now found a much nicer focus – her upcoming trip to Rome.

We may all at times experience different ways of feeling locked into certain thought patterns, but there is almost always a key. The trick is just finding the right key for this particular lock. Sometimes it could simply be that your mood level has gone down due to a tough week at work. In order to find the way back to your normal mood level, perhaps all you need is to be reminded of what makes you happy in life. Sometimes it is sufficient just talking to someone who cares for you to get back to your desired mood level.

The most important thing is to understand that we can feel good practically every single day. There is nothing, barring a few exceptions like tragedies and serious grief, that says you cannot feel good every day. When we bump into a bad day, we do not have to accept it. We may analyze this and ask ourselves: "Where do these feelings bogging me down come from? What do I have to do to get these feelings right and what can I do to feel good today?" Many times, it does not take all that much to get back to our desired state of mind. We have to learn how to guide ourselves towards finding this state of mind as often as possible.

When you identify which mood level you want to achieve under normal circumstances, you will also become able to notice when you drop below this level. You also come to understand that you do not have to accept bad days if you do not want to. You have figured out which tools you need to feel good, and you have figured out how to give yourself these tools. The next time you feel that your mood level is falling below your target level, stop and try to steer yourself back to the level you desire. Try to find methods and ways of thinking that work for you. If, for instance, you feel that you are uninspired at work, ask yourself: "What would give me inspiration at this very moment?" Maybe it would be helpful to give yourself something to look forward to. Maybe it would be helpful to use some kind of a reward as motivation. You may, for example, ask yourself: "If I reward myself with having half a bar of chocolate and watching a movie when I get home tonight, would that give me the right kind of fuel to be inspired today?"

Imagine sitting at home on your couch on a Sunday afternoon. You are bored and the anxiety of having to go to work tomorrow has you in its firm grip. What do you do in a situation like this? In this situation, you have every opportunity in the world to feel really good. You have had time off and you may have the whole afternoon to be with your family or doing anything you like. Do not accept that your thoughts are drifting away and creating unpleasant feelings about a new week of work about to start. Ask yourself what you need to do to avoid this feeling of anxiety and boredom next Sunday.

Imagine that your boss calls you into her office. She is in a bad mood, and in a serious voice, she criticizes you (unfairly, in your view). How do you handle a situation like that? Most people will allow themselves to get annoyed, upset or angry, which immediately will lower their mood level. If this happens to you, stop and give yourself time to process the situation. The fact of the matter is that everyone can learn to let these kinds of everyday nuisances blow away like dust.

The next time you are attacked by an everyday nuisance, stop and deal with what is causing you to be annoyed, and then try to get back to your desired state of mind.

"If you can't laugh because you don't feel happy,
then you can laugh to become happy."

15
The art of being able to handle your feelings

Your negative feelings are traces of earlier experiences or wounds. Your feelings may take control over you and come to rule your life. But, you also have the possibility of taking control over your own feelings.

Some feelings will never go away. They will always remain in your subconscious mind. What you can do is finding a way to handle them so that they do not end up controlling your life. The feelings will always have control over you until you learn how to deal with them. If you deny or suppress a negative feeling, then it will keep floating around, simmering until it one day explodes. More and more people today suffer from anxiety. This happens when the brain gets stuck in disturbing thought patterns. During a lifetime, about one in four will suffer from anxiety. Psychotherapists say that you can see a big difference between people who suffer from severe and mild anxiety. The difference is that those who suffer from severe anxiety have dealt with their feelings by suppressing them.

Everything in this world needs some kind of care. Plants need water or they wither away. Animals need food or they die. Material objects, like cars or houses, need to be maintained or else they fall into disrepair. For the exact same reason, we need to care for our feelings. If we do not, then our feelings will get sick and broken. You cure infections in the body with antibiotics, and you cure infections in the soul by caring for your feelings.

What is a feeling?

Defining a feeling is hard, but putting it in simple terms, you could say that it is a state of mind that may range all the way from happy to sad or angry. People are born with something called basic affects or, in simple terms, basic feelings, which are our basic emotional responses. Most scientists say that we have nine basic affects. These, according to American psychologist Silvan S. Tomkins, may be divided into three different groups:

Positive affects: interest – excitement and enjoyment – happiness
Neutral: surprise – startle
Negative: anger – rage, fear – terror, distress – anguish, shame, disgust and "dissmell"

Our feelings are our inner voice telling us how we feel. They tell us what we need to feel good and they tell us when something is wrong. Your feelings are your messengers and they are constantly bringing you messages. They want to tell you that something is good or bad. If you ignore them, then they will keep returning, understandably somewhat more annoyed and agitated, since they have previously been ignored and suppressed by you.

It is possible for everyone to practice dealing with their feelings in order to become their friend. There is a tool in cognitive behavioral therapy that you can use. This tool is referred to as SOAL, which stands for Stop, Observe, Accept and Let go.

Stop

Suppressed feelings and being in denial are things that ordinarily take place in our subconscious mind. The first step when dealing with unpleasant feelings is to stop and becoming aware of them. I would, however, like to point out that it may sometimes be necessary to get help at a deeper level by a friend or a therapist if we have a lot of suppressed feelings or live in denial to a large degree.

A feeling may often sneak up on you and then it is very easy to just push it aside. For some reason, we often want to avoid discovering feelings we believe will have a negative impact on our mood. So, as a display of pure survival instinct, we lie to ourselves and deny certain feelings. But keep in mind that it often takes more energy denying and suppressing unpleasant feelings than facing them in order to get rid of them.

Everyone has feelings they are not particularly proud of, but when we have the courage to bring out these kinds of feelings into the open, we grow as people. This gives us the possibility to change.

When we experience an unpleasant feeling, it is a common reaction to subconsciously push it aside, replacing it with a completely different feeling we do not even really need. What we are doing here is that we deny the unpleasant feeling and instead subconsciously focus on satisfying a much easier feeling. Here is an example: You are sitting at home watching a movie, when something in the plot creates an unpleasant feeling inside of you. You push this feeling aside, but something still feels wrong. You think to yourself: "I guess I'm hungry," so you go into the kitchen and get yourself a snack, even though you are actually not hungry. Or you think: "I need a bit of fresh air," so you step outside for a bit. Or you pick up your cellphone to check something out, even though you do not need to. Maybe you want to go out for a run, or you want to lie down, even though you are not tired. Subsequently, you trick the unpleasant feeling and it feels better for the moment. But the feeling is not stupid – it will return and then with more force and determination.

There is a risk when suppressing feelings, and that is that they may take on completely new forms further down the road. A suppressed feeling may take on a brand new disguise and manifest itself where it definitely does not belong. If you have suppressed difficult feelings from your childhood, then they may resurface in a completely new shape when you have a family of your own.

I would say that every time we push a feeling aside, we push ourselves a little bit further away from who we really are. If we make it a habit to push feelings aside and live in denial, then we are also pushing ourselves towards having a false self-image. The feelings have tried, on a number of occasions, to convey a message and if we ignore the message, we ignore ourselves. The message could be about things we have done wrong or conflicts, thoughts, anxieties, fears or actions that do not correspond with who we are. I would say that if we miss important information about ourselves too many times, then there is a risk that we lose ourselves as a person. In that case, it becomes much more difficult to find out what we really need to feel good. There is a good chance that we put ourselves in situations and settings that do not match our personality and values. We will feel this, and our feelings will go on shouting out their messages.

Observe

After you have stopped, you simply start to observe the unpleasant feeling. When the feeling manifests itself, practice observing it without assigning it any value. Be satisfied with only *seeing* the feeling. Put yourself outside of the feeling, instead of trying to penetrate it. This view is often clearer and more nuanced. To simplify the process of understanding the feeling, describe it to a friend or to yourself. When you understand what the feeling is trying to tell you, you also become more aware of how and why it affects you the way it does.

Accept

When you have stopped and observed the feeling, you need to learn how to accept it. If you succeed in doing this, you will be free from it and instead of having the feeling that it is ruling your life, it will become your friend.

Psychosynthesis, which is a well-recognized form of self-realization psychology, says that: "I *have* my feelings, but I *am* not my feelings."

Let go

When you have gone through these three steps, it is absolutely crucial that you learn how to let go of the feeling. Using this tool to cope with them, you will either become free of the feelings after having accepted them, or you will have new insights regarding necessary changes or actions. Since you have dealt with an unpleasant feeling, it is a good idea to focus on the things that will make you feel good there and then. This will hopefully help you achieve a sense of inner balance. There is no reason to keep dwelling on the feeling. Now is the time for you and the feeling to say goodbye. Instead, do something nice for yourself – you're worth it.

Your feelings originate in your brain. Thoughts and feelings travel along the same neural pathways in the brain. The feelings travel much faster and maybe that is why they sometimes take over our thoughts. The very fact that they use the same pathways in the brain sometimes makes it hard to separate a thought from a feeling. British literature professor and writer John Churton Collins once said: "Half our mistakes in life arise from feeling where we ought to think, and thinking where we ought to feel."

Identifying a feeling is about eliminating possible threats to our well-being, which may somewhere along the road have an adverse effect on our mood. Being honest with ourselves and our own feelings makes it easier to find inner peace. The better we get at connecting with our feelings, the more complete and genuine we will most likely become as individuals.

Instead of running away from the feeling that comes to you bearing a message, try stopping and listening to it. Try to really *see* the feeling, without evaluating it. It is better if you do this now, because otherwise you will have to do it later, and then the feeling has probably grown stronger and most likely evolved into something much more complicated. I would argue that it is the very process of running away from our feelings that gives them the nourishment necessary to grow.

The kind of self-awareness you build by being emotionally conscious will also help you to prevent unpleasant and negative feelings. This is by giving you the chance to prepare yourself mentally for situations you know will be particularly emotional, as well as by making it possible for you to steer clear of situations you know will be emotionally harmful to you.

Feelings come from within you and not from the outside world. What this means is that you cannot blame someone else for causing you to have an unpleasant feeling. I can fully sympathize with the fact that you may have experienced a plethora of bad things in your life. Maybe you were treated unfairly, maybe you had a rough childhood, but the feeling itself is created inside of you and no one else can decide whether or not you let this feeling continue controlling your behavior and therefore your life. At this moment in time, there is only one person who is responsible for your feelings and that person is You.

"It's not that I'm so smart, it's just that I stay with problems longer."

Albert Einstein

16
Forget about your age

What happens inside of us when we think about our age? How does thinking about getting older affect us? Consciously or subconsciously, we categorize ourselves as to what we should be like or not. Instead of focusing our thoughts on how we feel in our hearts, we focus on our actual age, which often stands in the way of us living life to the fullest.

How does thinking about our age benefit us? What is our attitude to aging and how does aging affect us as people? To delve into this subject, I had 100 persons in various ages interviewed. Something everyone had in common was that we all see more advantages in getting older when we are really young. Our birthdays are a big deal when we are kids. We can get a driver's license when we turn 16. We can vote when we turn 18 and we can buy alcohol when we turn 21.

My study indicated a fair amount of benefits with getting older all the way until 25. After that, the perception was that it was not all that beneficial getting older. On the other hand, the group was able to find many negative aspects with getting older, like the body deteriorating, having less energy, becoming less curious, less joy for life, less able to deal with stress, less spontaneity, having less fun, laughing less, putting hobbies aside and seeing your health declining. The study showed that after the age of 25, the mere thought of age and that we will get even older is exclusively associated with negative feelings.

As we all know, life is made up of many different phases and for many of us the life cycle looks something like this: When we are five, we play and we laugh. Life is all about having fun, exploring and learning things. Later, during puberty, we start to think more, we want to become more free and independent. We then experience a phase when we like to party with our friends. We are enjoying ourselves and think that clubs and pubs are what makes life worth living. Life moves along, and we get an education. Then we travel and explore the world. Perhaps we stay abroad for a short period of time.

Then comes the day when we feel that we have to grow up. We want to get a job, an apartment or a house and meet a life partner. Many in their 30s start thinking about having children and we tend to get stressed if we have not yet met our life partner. Later, as we get older, we may experience one or more crises. We live a family life and later the kids leave the nest. We are in our 50s and all of a sudden we realize that we want to have fun. We want to fulfill ourselves, travel and experience all kinds of adventures. The years go by, and eventually the body will start to act up. The energy level decreases and the fun moments are less and less common. Many people think: "I can't do that – I'm 60 years old for God's sake" or "That time has already passed, I live on my memories."

There is absolutely nothing wrong with living our lives according to these different phases. The problem, however, is that many people live according to this life cycle just because these phases correspond to one's age. Instead of guiding our goals, dreams and thoughts according to what the heart tells us we *want* to do, age often guides us towards acting the way we *should* do. The expectations of others tell us what we *should* be like and how we *should* live our life. Hence, we limit ourselves to not living life to the fullest throughout our whole lives. We limit ourselves more than we need to. If, for instance, you want to go out dancing when you are in your 60s, can you then think of one relevant reason for why you shouldn't? If your heart is telling you to go out and have a good time, then that is exactly what you should do. Do not let the norms of what is right and wrong stop you. If you are single, in your 30s, and feel stressed about not having any kids, consider whether being stressed is beneficial to you. Probably not. Being stressed is probably nothing but an obstacle for you. If having kids is in your cards, then you will have kids. I know that it is very hard thinking along these lines, but try shifting your focus from having children to instead meeting someone to share your life with. Because if you want to have children, then you also want to give this child both a good mom and a good dad.

When we think about our age, we often generate thoughts like: "I shouldn't be out dancing. I should grow up. I should have a family. I should make more money.

I should have come further than this in life. I should have a better job." These kinds of thoughts create a sense of stress, which in turn could create hang-ups. But do you know what the beautiful part is? There is nothing you should do or be like if you do not want to yourself. You do not have to grow up or get a family if you do not want to. There is really only one thing you should do, and that is to listen to your own inner voice and let your heart guide you.

The Dalai Lama said: "I believe that the very purpose of life is to be happy." When we create our lives according to what we should do, and life is lived according to what we should be like, it becomes very hard for us to be happy. In order for us to create genuine long-term happiness, life needs to come from within ourselves and not from the outside world.

When you think about getting older, it also influences your sense of well-being. It is hard not to constantly think about what we should be like, because, regardless of our age, we are constantly fed with information on what life should be like, what we should be like and how we should feel, regardless of age. If you are 35 and do not yet have children, then those around you will look at you and wonder if it really isn't about time. When you are 70, you hear how bad everyone around you feels and how worn out many people feel. It is all too easy for you to think it is simply due to your age on the days when you feel tired. Sure, age does matter, but if you think that your age is making you tired often enough, then you teach yourself that being tired is a part of getting older. It does not have to be like this though, because even if you are 70, your physical age could be 30 or it could be that you feel like 18 in your heart. If you frequently feel tired or depressed, then maybe it is due to something completely different. Perhaps there is something you can do to boost your energy or to feel happier. The fact that you had so much more energy when you were young does not have to be because you were younger. It could be because you used to fill your life with more things that boosted your energy.

I often get to hear that I am fortunate only being 39 years old and that I should enjoy my youth, because once I hit 50, things will start to deteriorate. I can choose to listen to this, or I can go on enjoying my relative youth and discard the thoughts that things may start to go south when I turn 50. There is a definite danger listening to talk like this, and that is that I may become very observant about the things that get worse when I turn 50. I can choose to either focus on the things about my health that are worse, or I can choose to focus on the things that are still good.

As we get older, our bodies tend to become less resilient than when we were young. This makes us trying to sense how we feel more than we did when we were young. The more we try to sense how we feel, the worse we will feel. Look for things not working as they should, and you are guaranteed to find them. Quite the reverse, you will find the things that work just fine in your body when you choose to focus on these. Try sensing what feels really good about your body right now, like your arms, the left leg, the belly, your heart, your hands, the ears, the eyes, the fingers and your calves. You will be surprised by just how many parts of your body actually feel good.

A number of years ago, I was talking to an old couple who were both in their 90s. The man started twisting and turning, he sighed and said: "Yikes, everything was just so much better before." His wife gave him a troubled, but loving look and replied: "No, dear, things were not better before – you were."

Studies from all over the world show that people feel their absolute worst when they are 46 years old. But then it turns around, and many are at their happiest after turning 60. For some, the opposite may be true. When they get older, they live their life as if it is – for all intents and purposes – already over. They quit working, some of their friends may pass away and they do not make any new friends. They get lonely and, for some strange reasons, they stop doing pleasant and fun things. They are satisfied simply watching TV or perhaps taking a walk. They say that they simply do not have the energy to do fun stuff anymore. But isn't it a fact that fun stuff, in particular, boost your energy? Even older people can travel, dance, sing, exercise, play chess, play around with a jumping rope, laugh out loud, be in love, throw money around or whatever the case may be. Ask yourself what makes you happy today and if you are doing these things frequently enough. Ask yourself if you can create an existence that makes you feel really good every day.

In some places on earth, people have no idea how old they are. They live as if age does not matter and they see no point in keeping track of how many years have passed since they were born. I would venture to say that we have two different ages that matter to us. You have your intellectual age, which, essentially, should get better the older you get, as you get more knowledge and life experience. Then we have your mental age, which is the age you have in your heart. The age on your driver's license, on the other hand, only acts as a reminder of all the things we should be or do. It also reminds us that we are getting closer to death. I think that many people have thought to themselves: "Wow, I've lived half of my life. Where have all the years gone by? Man, time certainly goes by quickly." We really should discard our "driver's license age" – it does not tell us anything.

Just as we age on the outside, we also age on the inside. We devote a lot of energy trying to look as young as possible. Almost everyone over the age of 30 gets very happy hearing that they look younger than they really are. The question, though, is what is the most important: a young exterior or a young interior? Scientists claim that people with a young mind are healthier and happier than those who, as they grow older, also grow older on the inside. We know that a lot of people put a great deal of energy into rejuvenating their exterior, but how much time do we really spend trying to rejuvenate our interior?

When we undertook our study on age, we asked the participants whether it is important to remain young at heart. 99% answered that this is very important. We also found the factors that help people retaining a young interior.

Below, the results of the study are presented, with the most common answer at the top, followed by number two and so on:

- *My children*
- *Music*
- *Love*
- *Experiencing nature*
- *Keeping a sense of curiosity and creating new interests*
- *A healthy lifestyle, encompassing regular exercise, a good diet and good habits*
- *Keeping the brain occupied and learning new things*
- *Friends in all ages*
- *Outdoor activities*
- *Humor*
- *Pleasure in all forms*
- *Dealing with unpleasant and hurt feelings*

One thing that surprised me and made me extra curious, was the fact that music was so high up on the list. What is it about music that keeps our spirits young? Swedish professor emeritus and stress researcher Töres Theorell says that music passes by the reasoning parts of the brain straight into the emotional brain. From there, a lot of processes can be initiated – processes that affect how we feel. Theorell also says that research shows that we produce more of the oxytocin hormone when we listen to music. Oxytocin relieves pain and anxiety and provides us with a sense of peace and quiet. This substance also assists the body when repairing worn-out cells. Music, furthermore, releases the body's own happiness hormone, endorphins. Apart from music stimulating your brain cells, which in turn release hormones that are very beneficial to you, it can also help you in other ways. For example, music can help you to fall asleep. It lowers and counteracts stress and it can help you to have more effective and longer workouts. Listening to music is about transmitting feelings, which is why it has such a tremendously positive effect on us.

Ellen Langer, professor in psychology at Harvard, has undertaken an experiment where a group of 80-year-old men got to live as if they were 20 years younger. To make the transformation as realistic as possible, they were isolated in a building where everything was arranged the same way as 20 years earlier. Furniture, magazines, movies and news were switched out. They were no longer given the assistance

80-year-olds are normally entitled to, but were expected to make do just as well as 60-year-olds. During the course of this experiment, the men started to change their views on what was possible for them. Before the start of the experiment, they were stumbling along, but at its conclusion they were playing soccer. They no longer considered themselves to be 80 years old. Instead, they had throughout the experiment come to raise their expectations as to what was possible.

The results of this experiment was that the participants got better posture, as well as better memory and hearing. If you are 80 and expect to have trouble walking, then you will have a harder time walking. If you are 80 and expect to feel like someone who is 60, then you will feel more like a 60-year-old. Scientists say that people can do much more than they think they can. Our expectations when it comes to ourselves determine how much we will be able to do.

In normal eye exams, the letters go from being big to being smaller and smaller. This creates an expectation that it will soon be difficult to make out the letters. In an experimental eye exam, they started with the smallest letters, which then got bigger and bigger. The test group then got a better result. When the letters got bigger, the people in this group expected to be able to see soon, which improved their result. If we expect to succeed in something, then it is more likely that we will succeed. Just the same, our chances of success decrease if we expect to fail. Our expectations concerning ourselves set limits for what we can do.

Imagine what a great feeling it would be to think: "I feel like I'm 20 and if I want to be 20, then I can be 20." You are free to be exactly how you feel. Of course, everyone feels tired and old sometimes, but in that case, enjoy the days when you feel alert and brimming with energy even more. Do not limit yourself by thinking that you are old. What I am trying to say is that growing old is something very beautiful, but, regrettably, aging is perceived by many as something negative.

We have different needs throughout the different phases of life. The things that made us happy when we were 18 may not make us happy today, but it could also be the case that exactly the same things make us happy today as when we were 18. In that case, do not let yourself be held back just because it is not appropriate for your current age. If you let your heart find the paths in your life, then I promise you that you will become even happier. If you let your age guide your choices, then you will be cheated. Focusing on your age will lead you in the wrong direction and this kind of focus will set out traps for you. This focus will construct obstacles for you and it will trip you when you want to reach your dreams.

17
Find that great love for yourself

When you find that great love for yourself, you find more than just the love for others – you also find a love for life.

You could say that self-esteem comes from the inside and is about how you esteem yourself, whereas self-confidence comes from the outside and is about your faith in your own abilities. They are both obviously just as important, but it is necessary to separate the two in order to better develop them individually. Self-esteem is about what you *are* and self-confidence is about what you *do*. Children are often told how good they are when they accomplish something: "You were

really good today on the soccer field. You're such a good kid having washed the dishes and made your bed. You're so good in school." From an early age, children are taught that they are good when they perform. This is all good, but we also need to teach them that they are good when they are not doing anything in particular. If a kid is only told that she is good when she achieves something, then there is a risk that she develops good self-confidence, but not as good self-esteem.

Having low self-esteem contributes to behaviors and thoughts that tend to create a lot of unwelcome feelings, which, in turn, create obstacles on the path of life. Having good self-esteem makes you completely aware of your own intrinsic value. You do not need to perform to know that you are good – you know that you are good just the way you are. Having good self-esteem makes you put yourself in situations that make you feel good since you know that you are worth it. This builds a sense of safety and inner harmony. Having good self-esteem is important for the kind of dreams you will fulfill. It is impossible for you to dream big dreams if you cannot see your own value. In order to have big dreams and to be able to live your life to the fullest, you need to understand and feel that you are actually worth it.

Everyone can learn to understand their own value and thus strengthen their own self-esteem, and there are many areas where we can work on strengthening our self-esteem.

Where does your bad self-esteem come from?

If you are not completely satisfied with your sense of self-esteem, ask yourself why that is. If you really put in the effort, you will find the answers even though they may be buried deep below the surface. Through reasoning and finding out the underlying causes, it will become easier for you to get a grasp on what you need to do to strengthen your self-esteem. It works sort of the same way as with allergies. When you know what you are allergic to, you can give yourself what you need to be able to cope with the allergy. Being aware means putting yourself in situations where you feel good, while making it possible for you to grow in situations where you feel less good.

Dealing with mistakes

It is impossible for someone who wants to live his life to the fullest and make his dreams come true to not make a few mistakes along the way. Mistakes are a part of life, in a sense, and they provide you with nourishment for your personal growth.

Making a mistake is not a failure, but not learning from one's mistakes is certainly a wasted opportunity for gaining knowledge.

A total failure, in this context, would be to try to steer clear of disappointments and mistakes. The only way of living your life to the fullest is to look upon these as a natural part of life. Instead, aim to learn from them and to deal with them the best you can.

Acceptance

A basic principle when trying to build a strong sense of self-esteem is to forgive and to accept that time has gone by. Just the same way you are trying to come to accept the flaws and imperfections in those around you, you also need to do the same for your own. This does not mean that you should stop growing – it means that you should accept yourself as being human.

Good deeds

There is a strong correlation between your self-esteem and your conscience. If you do something that has a negative impact on someone else, then you will most likely end up with a guilty conscience and this will lower your sense of self-esteem. If, on the other hand, you do something that has a positive impact on someone else, then you will provide your conscience with a nice feeling, which, in turn, will strengthen your sense of self-esteem. What this means is that if you hurt someone, then you also hurt yourself, and if you are nice to someone, then you are also nice to yourself.

Showing empathy, being considerate and doing good deeds is a wonderful way to strengthen your own self-esteem. You do not need a reason for helping others – help them because you want to. To get started doing good deeds, you may decide that you will for one week do at least three good deeds every day. Let someone ahead of you in line at the grocery store. If the little boy getting an ice cream does not have enough money – give him enough change to buy it. Wait and hold the door open. Give someone you bump into an unexpected compliment or why not help someone out in traffic. Get out there and try it already today!

18 years ago, I had just bought my first car and, in all the excitement, I forgot to get gas. I was barely 20 years old and I was very worried about how I was to solve my fuel situation. I called the nearest gas station, which was five miles away, and I can still clearly remember the lady who answered saying: "I'll fill up a small jerry can for you and I'll be there in 15 minutes." I will always remember this good deed.

Every time I see this lady, who is now in her 70s, I light up as a sun and I get all warm inside thinking about how she helped me that one time.

Raise your gaze towards the world. Think about how you can take part in improving it. There are many things you can dedicate your efforts to, like world hunger, animal protection or environmental issues. Why not look around in your closest surroundings? Is there someone who needs your support, or could you help someone to make a dream come true? Also consider how you want those around you to treat you and then start treating them the same way.

Remember the following: kindness is contagious. When you are kind to someone, then this kindness will tend to rub off so that this person in turn is kind to someone in her surroundings. Your kindness will spread to a lot more people than the person you are helping out at the moment.

Follow your own values

Your values are at the core of everything you do and going against your own values will have a negative impact on your self-esteem. Following your values will also have an impact on your self-esteem, but a positive one.

Live your own life

Your life on this planet is very short. Be careful that you plan and live the life you want to live. Way too many people get stuck within the confines of how they are expected to live. Just because everyone else is turning right does not automatically mean that you should also make the same turn. You have been given the gift of life, so treasure this gift and make sure to live it the way you want to. Seek the answers within yourself. How do you want to live your short life on this planet?

Give your inner procrastinator more space

A lot of people have a hard time not doing anything. They feel like a waste of space when they are doing nothing in particular. If you want to spend your whole weekend on the couch, then do so. You probably have some reasons for needing that extra time to relax. If you do not have a reason, do it anyway for no other reason than that this is what you want to do. You are just as good when you do nothing. Practice simply being.

Confront your "inner critic"

Why do you sometimes have negative thoughts about yourself? Are they valid and are you being fair to yourself? Would you judge your loved ones as harshly as you judge yourself? You are definitely not getting away with criticizing yourself without providing a reasonable explanation. Confront yourself and demand an explanation.

Practice having nice thoughts about yourself

Frequently, we are very good at focusing our attention on the things we are not so good at. Even when we have been really good for 95% of the day, it is often easy to choose to focus on the remaining 5%, when things did not go so well. When you focus on these 5%, you put yourself down, which in the long run will suck the life force out of you. The fact that you do not perform that well during 5% of your day is actually only proof that you are human, just like everyone else, and with all kinds of flaws and imperfections. Try replacing the harsh and belittling thoughts with nice and loving ones.

If you practice focusing on all the positive things you *are* and the things you *do* frequently enough, then you will eventually get really good at it.

Acknowledge the value of both accomplishments and inner qualities

It is usually easier to be acknowledged for accomplishments and it is usually easier to feel good about ourselves after we have done something good. When it comes to our inner qualities, however, we often need to work a bit more. If there is no one around you acknowledging your inner qualities, then do so yourself. Let yourself know that you are a good person, a great listener, kind, considerate, emotional, smart, pleasant and empathetic. These are amazing qualities, which you should remind yourself of each and every day. Try finding a balance between appreciating your accomplishments and appreciating your inner qualities.

Create a fan list

Sit down and take your time considering what you appreciate and admire in others. Consider your family, your friends, people you have only ever seen on TV, people from times past and people you meet in your everyday life. Make sure that you have enough time to be thorough and to write down carefully analyzed traits. You probably already possess many of the traits you find, but don't worry about that.

Write down as many traits as possible – the longer the list, the better. When the list is complete, you have a list of who you want to be.

The search for acknowledgment

Humans have lived through a lot of different eras – all the way from the Stone Age and the Iron Age to the IT Age. The question, though, is if we are presently living in the "Acknowledgement Age," and also whether this is a good era for our future evolution. The question is whether it is a good thing to "chase" and actively seek acknowledgment through the present-day social media landscape. Does this kind of affirmation mean that we are looking for a long-term effect or, rather, does it create some kind of a void? We humans have a number of different reasons for seeking affirmation. There is nothing wrong with that per se, but it is important that we try to understand why we do this. Many people primarily use social media to seek affirmation. For many, it is even about creating a feeling of *existing*.

In order for acknowledgements to have a more long-term effect, they need to come more naturally and not through calling out - *see me!* If you tend to seek

affirmation, think about why you seek this kind of affirmation and what will happen to your inner feelings if you stop seeking it. Are there other things you can do long-term to replace this feeling?

Create a kind diary

If you find yourself in a phase where you really want to strengthen your self-esteem, then you will find that it is very beneficial to create a diary where you only write kind things about yourself. Create a new habit in your life, where you every night devote a few minutes for reflection on what has been good about yourself during the day. Perhaps, you have been nice to someone, made someone happy or done something good at work. Also write down when you have received positive feedback from someone around you. Remember to be generous towards yourself. Writing a "kind diary" naturally gives you time to focus your thoughts on the things that are good about you. During the days when your self-esteem goes down somewhat, you can always take out your kind diary and remind yourself of how good you are.

Setting up goals

Completing small goals strengthens both your self-esteem as well as your self-confidence. These goals could be about anything from work-related goals to goals concerning possible bad habits, like being late or eating too much candy. You may also use the list you wrote about the kind of traits you appreciate in others and use it to set goals for yourself. Choose one trait at a time and then start working on it until you are satisfied.

Confront your fears

Everyone has, or has had, fears, although a lot of people have not identified them yet. What are you afraid of? Write down the things that scare you and put them down on your list of goals. Then start working your way down the list, fear by fear, and soon you will be completely rid of them. When you have conquered a fear, take out your kind diary and describe how you felt when doing so.

Reward yourself

You have hundreds of reasons for rewarding yourself. You may reward yourself for having the courage to take on a fear. You may reward yourself for having dealt with a difficult feeling or for being nice to someone. If you do something you find difficult, then I think that you definitely deserve a reward. Why not reward yourself when you have allowed yourself to just be for a whole evening? When you reward yourself, you give yourself a nice kind of acknowledgement, which, in turn, strengthens both your self-esteem and your self-confidence. Furthermore, you activate the reward system in your brain, which then releases substances that make you feel good.

Activate your brain's reward system

When you do something you like, the reward system in your brain is activated and you release the brain's own feeling-good substances. Spending time with someone you like, laughing, having fun, having a nice meal or exercising are some of the things that trigger the reward system in your brain. Activating your reward system has a positive impact on your self-esteem.

Gratitude

When you display and feel gratitude in all its forms, you strengthen yourself and this has a positive influence on your sense of self-esteem. Gratitude towards yourself and others, towards life and all of its gifts. Gratitude towards the things many take for granted, like health, having food on the table, your home and birds singing. When you are having nice thoughts about someone, then remember to tell this person. Let people you like or feel gratitude towards know how you feel.

Socialize with the "right" people

Spend time with people who make you feel good and who give you the right kind of nourishment. People who really appreciate you for who you are and who always respect you. Spending time with the "right" people makes it easier for you to feel accepted, appreciated and safe.

Do things that make you happy

When you find yourself in situations that make you happy, you automatically become a better person. This, in turn, strengthens your sense of self-esteem.

Get interested in yourself

Develop an interest in yourself as a person. Inside of you is a goldmine of exciting information – things like undiscovered passions, mysterious hang-ups, strange feelings that have a negative impact on you, hidden talents or fun and interesting sides of you that have not as of yet been allowed to blossom. This interest in yourself creates a sense of curiosity, which helps building your self-esteem. This will then make you more aware of what you need in order to feel good as often as possible.

A strong sense of self-awareness makes it possible for you to always give yourself the best, which in the long run improves your self-esteem.

Become your own best friend

You are the most important person in your life. If you are functioning well, then you will also function well together with your family, friends and colleagues, as well as with everyone around you in general. Do you agree with the notion that the more you like someone, the nicer you get towards this person? At the same time, you may sometimes show coldness, arrogance, or indifference to people you do not like.

This means the following: The more you like yourself, the warmer, the nicer and the better you will also treat yourself. The by far most important relationship you will ever get to experience is your relationship with yourself. Try building a friendship with yourself that is so good that you become your own best friend.

Alone time

You also have to give yourself enough time to nurture the relationship with yourself. Maybe you have so much to do that it is not possible for you to give yourself any alone time. In that case, my suggestion is that you create the necessary space and time to look after yourself. This will be one of your best time investments ever. Try creating moments when you laugh and have a good time by yourself. When you can enjoy your own company, then you have come a long way towards having a better sense of self-esteem.

18
The art of believing in yourself

Having a strong sense of self-esteem makes you feel good and fills your inner self with harmony and a sense of feeling safe. Being self-confident opens up a whole world of opportunities. Your sense of self-confidence has an enormous impact on the people you meet. If you perceive yourself as troublesome, complicated or ignorant, then that is exactly the feeling you transmit to the receiver. If not even you believe in yourself, how do you expect others to believe in you?

When you give yourself a good sense of self-confidence, your life changes. If you believe in your own abilities, then you tend accept opportunities offered to you and you also have more courage to think much bigger. The benefit of having big thoughts is that you subconsciously open yourself up for big events. Having a good sense of self-confidence makes you less scared of failing and builds your inner strength. You increase your chances of getting to live the life you want to live, and not ending up being limited by how those around you think you should live. Always wanting to be yourself comes naturally to you and, furthermore, you will feel proud of the unique individual you really are.

Believing in yourself is a priceless asset, but no matter how hard we try, it is hard to build this faith. Building self-confidence is kind of like trying to complete a large jigsaw puzzle. First, you decide to buy a certain jigsaw puzzle and then you put all of the pieces on a table, all mixed together. Then you start the process of sorting the pieces. You look at them and start putting them where you think they belong in the picture. A certain piece may be extra difficult – it needs special attention – but after some effort you figure it out and you can move on to the next piece. The more you get to know the pieces and the more you work with them, the easier it gets to later make them fit into the complete picture of the puzzle. Sometimes you get stuck and things may feel somewhat hopeless, but this is precisely when it could be enough just to figure out one single piece. If you succeed in doing this, many other pieces may fall into place as well. Just having one piece falling into place may be enough for you to get the strength to carry on all the way to the finish line.

Everyone has the ability to build a strong sense of self-confidence, but it requires a conscious effort. Below follows a few tips, as well as traps, I hope will inspire you to find your own pieces of the puzzle towards better self-confidence.

Stop caring what others think

All too many push themselves aside in order to try to satisfy the needs of those around them. Instead of focusing on what they need to do to feel good, they focus their attention on being well-liked. Someone once said: "Do not try to change yourself to be liked by others. Be yourself and the right people will come to like you." Stop caring what others think of you and instead keep in mind that your friends like you just the way you are. This obviously does not mean that you should stop giving the people around you the amount of respect they deserve – quite the opposite. By ceasing to focus on what others think of you, you create a greater space for you to really have the courage to be yourself all the way.

Get good at a hobby

Creating a feeling that you are good at something helps you on your journey towards a really good sense of self-confidence. Apart from improving your self-confidence by, for instance, being good in your profession, as a parent or by being a really good partner, it is also possible for you to build your self-confidence by getting good at a hobby. Enjoying a fun hobby while, at the same time, noticing that you develop and get better and better at it will have a positive impact on your self-confidence. There is usually something of a ripple effect when we notice that we are good at something. Often, we get to experience a feeling of: "If I can do this, then I may also succeed in doing all the other things on my mind."

A fair comparison

Comparing yourself with others is in most cases among the worst thing you can do for your sense of self-confidence. The reason for this is that we are almost always inclined towards comparing ourselves with someone we perceive to be better at this one particular thing. Curiously enough, you do not consider that you may be better than this person when it comes to a lot of other things. All of your attention is focused on this one particular aspect, which you perceive this person to master better than you.

A few years ago, I was coaching this massively goal-oriented salesperson. He worked as a telemarketer in a small office, which was part of a larger corporation. The first months working there, he did not feel all that good since he saw himself as a terrible salesperson. This was because he was comparing himself with the best salespeople in the office. Later, when he became the best salesperson at the office, he still thought of himself as being bad at selling things. Now he was comparing himself with the best salespersons in the district. And, when he became the number one salesperson in the district, he started comparing himself with the best salespersons in the country. There was always someone better and this led to his downfall. He had a brilliant career in his cards, but his propensity for always comparing himself with others gave him a feeling of never being good enough.

Making these kinds of comparisons rarely leads to anything positive. There are, however, exceptions when it may be beneficial to compare oneself with those who are better, like in elite level sports. Regardless, you need to find a balance so that you may, every once in a while, feel that you are really good at something.

A lecturer I once listened to in Toronto told us about a study showing that people who compare themselves with themselves have more fun, experience less performance anxiety, enjoy life more and have more realistic expectations when it comes to themselves.

Act as *if* you have a strong sense of self-confidence

Everything you want to improve and develop requires practice. One way of practicing your self-confidence is by studying someone you know with a good sense of self-confidence. Study which kind of attributes this person is transmitting indicating that she is self-confident. If there is no one in your surroundings who seems to have a good sense of self-confidence, then read up on the most common signs of having this. Thereafter, you try to act in a similar way – similar to how a self-confident person acts.

The best way to learn how to do something is to do it yourself, and here is your chance to do just that. Initially, it may feel somewhat phony, but it will eventually come to you more naturally and then those around you will hopefully perceive you as someone with good self-confidence. When those around you start to think of you in this way, then your own sense of having good self-confidence will be further strengthened.

The purpose of this exercise is to give you the opportunity to practice transmitting good self-confidence, but also to inspire you to put in the effort required to building this for yourself. Self-confidence may take many different forms and shapes, and through practice and effort you will eventually find your own way towards achieving this.

Fire the director

A lot of people have their own director in the sense that they are constantly analyzing themselves and their behavior and, if this was not enough, they also judge themselves. They are in other words extremely aware of what they are saying, how they express themselves and how they act while, simultaneously, judging themselves. People you meet often think: "I wonder what he's thinking about me right now. Why did I say that and how did I just come across?" The good news is that no one observes you as carefully as you do. That would be impossible, because they have themselves to consider and, accordingly, they do not notice your flaws or bad days in the same way that you do.

Learn to receive praise

Regardless of your confidence level, you get energized when you are praised. A lot of people brush off praise: "Eh, that was nothing special." Giving praise to some people is a lot like throwing a bouncing ball against a wall. As soon as the ball hits the wall, it is rapidly pushed away. This is a great shame, because when you receive praise, you actually get a small gift from that person. Throwing away a gift is a mean thing to do – both to yourself and to the person who gave it to you. Praising someone is a sweet gesture and we really ought to show our appreciation for those who give us praise. They have actually observed you doing something good and, apart from that, they are so nice that they tell you about this, probably expecting you to get happy.

If you have a hard time receiving compliments, ask yourself why. I know that there is an underlying cause for this and if you try to figure this out, then you will eventually learn how to receive these wonderful gifts from those around you. One good method for learning to receive praise is to really listen to compliments for a whole week, without brushing them off and later, when you are by yourself, write them down. Also practice complimenting yourself. Show yourself appreciation – both for who you *are* as well as for what you *do*. I promise you that some of the characteristics you perceive as ordinary are seen by others as beautiful. When you make your inner strengths visible to yourself, you also make them visible for those around you and, in that way, both you and the people in your vicinity get to enjoy the things that are good about you. When you take notice of your inner strengths and praise yourself, you also give yourself a sense of appreciation, which in the long run fills you with vitality.

Music

We must not underestimate the power of music. Many people claim that their level of self-confidence is increased when listening to certain kinds of music.

Stand tall and feel really good

When you feel fresh and at peace, you give yourself a more pleasant overall feeling. Consider the fact that your body plays a big part in how you feel at the moment. When you stand tall, you give your inner self a signal that you matter.

Think along the line of solutions

On life's journey we will bump into problems and make mistakes. This is a natural part of life. Instead of focusing all of your energies on the mistake or the problem itself, you get stronger by directing all of your energies towards rectifying the problem or even finding a solution. For example:

Situation: You make a mistake at work.
Your first reaction: "I certainly screwed up this time. Now, we'll lose all of this time and money. This is so annoying. What's the boss going to think and what will my colleagues say?"
Instead think: "How am I to rectify this mistake and what did I learn from this?"

Situation: You forget your passport when you and your wife are going away on vacation.
Your first reaction: "I'm such a moron! How could I be so stupid? I can't believe this – I've ruined the whole trip. I feel awful."
Instead think: "Alright, so I screwed up, but how do we solve this? Is there enough time for me to get back home and pick up the passport or is it possible to book a new flight?"

Situation: You get transferred at your job.
Your first reaction: "Does this mean that my boss isn't satisfied with my performance? This feels really tough. I liked my old job. Now, all of my sense of security is slipping right through my fingers. What's going to happen now?"
Instead think: "For a number of reasons, the company needs a new structure. It's going to be exciting to get to do new things! I just have to give it a bit of time before I learn how to do them and also get a chance to grow."

Situation: By mistake, you end up saying something hurtful to your girlfriend.
Your first reaction: "I just don't get myself sometimes. How could I be such a fool and say those idiotic things?"
Instead think: "Wow, that was just a really unfortunate thing I just said. What do I need to do to make this right?"

Break the ice

A relatively simple method for building confidence is to strike up unexpected conversations with new people. A good friend of mine has made it a habit to as often as possible start talking to strangers in his everyday life. When he is sitting on the bus, he takes out his box of breath mints and looks at the person across from him with his kind eyes, while asking: "May I offer you a mint?" He also rarely misses a chance to hold the door open for others. The fact that the person in question is 50 feet back makes no difference – he simply keeps standing there, waiting. If he sees a tourist holding a map, he will approach him and say: "Do you need any help finding the way?" This leads to a couple of minutes' worth of rewarding conversation, which leads to my friend feeling invigorated afterwards.

Speak slowly

When you speak slowly, you convey a feeling that what you are saying is important. You show that you are someone worth listening to and this affects how others perceive you. You grow as a person when those around you treat you with respect.

Become a doer

If you frequently talk about things you want to do at a later date, but which never materialize, your confidence level goes down. Conversely, being able to achieve what you set out to do strengthens your sense of self-confidence. One good method for becoming a doer is to consider whether there is something you have wanted to do for a long time. After that, you simply get it done without even reflecting on fears or other issues. You just do it.

Knowledge

Many people may be very confident in one area, while being quite insecure in another. It is, for example, possible for the same person to be very confident in her profession, somewhat confident playing golf and really insecure in social situations. That the level of confidence can shift depending on the context is almost always connected to this person's knowledge and experience. The more knowledge, the more confidence. If you feel insecure in certain situations, then you may reduce this feeling by raising your level of knowledge. Knowledge about upcoming travel destinations or upcoming job interviews and carefully preparing for that speech on Saturday. Knowledge and preparation creates a sense of security. Repetition and experience builds confidence.

Remember that taking small steps is sufficient and remember that many small steps eventually become a giant leap. Have an end goal that you are to live your life according to the principle that you are worth the absolute best, and do not settle for anything less. Keep in mind that you will fall along the way, but that this is really not a failure. The only thing that would be construed as a failure is if you would not get up again to continue on your journey.

19
Your thoughts guide your performance

The first step towards success is to succeed in your mind. The second step is to succeed in your heart.

Generating the thought that you will accomplish something is the easy part. But becoming convinced in your heart is much more difficult. In my view, this is a prerequisite for reaching your destination. You really have to feel it in your bones that you will succeed. When you have created this feeling, you have also created the foundation for reaching your desired goal. But how is one to do this? How do you create a feeling saying that there is no way you can't succeed?

Surround yourself with successful people

Somebody once said: "What one man can do, another can do."

When you see others achieving certain goals or results, something happens inside of you. Seeing someone else accomplishing the thing you dream of makes it seem possible for you as well. In the world of sports, there are a lot of examples of this phenomenon. During the 1980s, Swedish tennis seemed set on taking on the world. At one point, "tiny" Sweden had seven of its players ranked among the best 25 players in the world. Mats Wilander won the French Open. His practice buddies, who were sent home packing after the first round, started thinking: "I sometimes beat him during practice. That means that I should also be able to win." Later on, they too started winning competitions.

Looking at track and field, we find countless examples. There were boundaries that were deemed impossible to jump over, throw longer or run faster. Someone bursts this boundary and a number of other competitors see this, realize what is possible and then follow along. When we see someone else achieving the very thing we dream of, the brain gets a signal telling us that it really is possible. This signal works as a reminder, and with each time we get this reminder, it feels more natural that we will also succeed in doing this. Imagine surrounding yourself with people who keep on failing trying to do the things you dream of. Then you are constantly reminded of how extremely hard it is to succeed. The successes in your sport, of your club, of your friends or of your company create a ripple effect. If those around you succeed, a feeling is created saying that "if they can do it, so can I."

Imagine your success

Sit down somewhere calm and quiet and close your eyes. Think back to one point in life when you succeeded in doing something or when you performed really well. Try to remember how you felt during this moment of success. Bring this feeling along and start fantasizing about how you will reach your next goal or dream. Imagine how nice it will feel when you succeed. Open your eyes. I am certain that the feeling of your upcoming success has started to grow inside of you. This type of mental exercise is a very good method for preparing both mind and body for a certain performance or experience. It is also very common among top athletes. Right before the start, many athletes go through the match or competition in their minds. They construct a mental success image where they see themselves performing extremely well, while using an incredibly effective technique.

Scientists say that some parts of the brain are incapable of separating imagined events from real ones. This means that if the brain is thinking that "this can't be done," then impulses are sent out throughout the body that this is actually so – "this can't be done." Maybe you can relate to a situation at work when you have deemed something impossible and, inevitably, it turned out to be so. If you are playing tennis and, right before your second serve, you think: "What if I get a double fault?" Or, playing golf, you think: "What if I miss this important putt?" So, what do you think will happen? We always miss when thinking along these lines. When you think, your brain sees pictures, meaning that if you are thinking of missed putts or double faults, then that is exactly what your brain will see. When you fantasize about accomplishing things, you are simply tricking some parts of your brain into believing that you have already done so. According to French neurologist and brain expert Marc Jeannerod, a possible physiological explanation for why our thoughts play such a big role for how we will perform is that we use the same part of the brain when we think about the action as when we actually perform it.

What we need to do before every important situation, or when we want to perform as well as we possibly can, is to send out impulses that we will succeed. If we are to give ourselves the best possible chances for success, then we need to build a thought pattern that sends out these very impulses. Your brain simply needs to see pictures where you succeed.

Create a winning feeling

Many of the world's top athletes have one thing in common – they never consider the fact that they may actually fail or lose. They have created such a strong faith in themselves and in their own capabilities that they are incapable of imagining anything else but winning. Using our own thoughts, we are all capable of creating this feeling.

Consider what you would like to change in your life, or which dream you would pursue if you were guaranteed that there was no way you could fail. I am not able to give you this kind of a guarantee, but I can guarantee you the following: If you are able to think frequently enough that you will succeed, then this thought will create a feeling that will envelop you in a sense of conviction that everything else seems completely unlikely.

Undertake one tiny change each day

Sometimes we want to accomplish something that feels impossible. We want to, but we know that it is hard. We want to, but we are unable to create the feeling that we will succeed. Consider your desired accomplishment or desired goal once more. Is it possible to break it down into a number of intermediate goals? What do you need to do today, a week or a month from now for you to reach your desired goal in a year's time?

If you want to become twice as good in some area within a year, then it is possible for you to create a thought that you will succeed, but you are probably going to have a hard time convincing yourself of this deep down in your heart. Twice as good is a very ambitious goal. It feels very distant. If, on the other hand, you break it down to making one small improvement or some fine-tuning every day, then the goal will feel much more reasonable. Succeeding in doing this means that you will actually have carried out 365 small changes during this year.

Many years ago, when working as a tennis coach, one of my students approached me and told me that he wanted to become twice as good at playing tennis. I asked him why he had specifically chosen to become twice as good and he replied, somewhat embarrassed: "My friend is twice as good as I am, and I hate losing to him." He practiced with me three times a week and for each time our goal was to improve one small detail in his game. One time, for instance, he worked on being able to hit longer basic shots, and another time he tried to improve his footwork. The months passed by and one day he showed up for practice with a big grin on his face. His look said it all – he had defeated his friend.

A few years ago, I attended a lecture where the lecturer discussed a study analyzing how someone's life may be changed when undertaking a tiny change every day. Everyone was given the task of undertaking one small improvement in their lives each day. It could be stuff like having a difficult conversation with a friend or becoming more assertive in their daily lives. Regardless of where they started out, this study showed a definite increase in the quality of life for every participant.

Learn from others who have already reached the target

When you are on your way towards fulfilling your goals and dreams, it is often incredibly inspiring to spend time with someone working as kind of a mentor for you. If you do not have the opportunity to have a mentor in your life, then you may instead create role models in order to let them inspire you.

If someone accomplishes something, then maybe she knows something you do not. What does she know that you have not yet learned? Could it be that she has some kind of a system for being able to do this? If you do the same, will you accomplish the same, or do you have to make certain adjustments that will fit you better? People's accomplishments are not coincidental. Every success story has its own ingredients. Looking at others could give you the right guidance. If not, maybe it could inspire you to find your own ingredients. Consider which ingredients you need in order to be convinced that you will fulfill your goals and dreams.

20
Let your thoughts change your life

There are no situations that make us feel bad - what makes us feel bad is how we perceive the situation.

Many years ago, I was playing a very important tennis game in a prestigious Swedish youth tournament. I was seven years old and I simply loved playing tennis. But this particular day was not all that much fun. I was in a bad mood and I was about to face utter defeat. I was usually happy when playing tennis, but not this time. I was so mad that I once even threw my racket into a wall. During a break in the game towards the end, I sat down to have a drink of water. All of a sudden my dad appears and hands me a completely different water bottle. I found this quite odd, as I already had a bottle, but he was persistent and told me to use his bottle instead. I grabbed his bottle and was about to take a sip when I noticed that there were things written on the bottle: You're a good tennis player – You have a good forehand – You are fast – Have fun – and, at the very bottom – BE HAPPY! I remember finding the whole thing somewhat odd and I had a hard time figuring out why he had written all these affirmations on the bottle. But when I returned to the court, something truly remarkable had happened. My frustration was gone. It was more fun to play. My strokes were a little bit better and I felt happy. The game turned into a true nail-biter, which I ended up winning after having played for three hours.

As a seven-year-old, I had absolutely no idea what I had done to turn my extremely bad day around. Today I know exactly what happened. Reading the text on the water bottle, I saw mental images where playing tennis was fun. I saw mental images where I was in a good mood and where I played well. Seeing these images led me to subconsciously focus on the positive aspects and, consequently, my anger and frustration was blocked.

Your thoughts govern your feelings and if you can learn to control your thoughts, you will also be able to control your feelings.

Using your five senses, you interpret all the inputs running through your body and soul. Your interpretation is based on earlier events and life experiences, and it is crucial for how you see yourself and the world around you. Everyone experiences their own reality, which is based on their own interpretation. When you allow yourself to focus your thoughts on things that have a negative impact on you, then you will also attract negative experiences.

Everything begins with a thought and, subconsciously, your life will take the same route as your thoughts. Believing that life is hard will make your own view that life is hard all the more powerful. Believing that your body aches will make your experience of having an aching body all the more powerful.

Your feelings are almost always connected to your thoughts, and if you allow yourself to not have negative thoughts regarding a certain situation, then you will not experience this situation as all that difficult. Consider how you would react if you were to forget your cellphone on the train. Perhaps your first reaction would be along the lines of: "I can't believe this. The phone was more or less brand new and I have so much important stuff stored in it. What if it ends up in the wrong hands? Help!" Reactions like these lead to a long series of anxious thoughts, which, in turn, create bad feelings.

Another way to approach this situation would be: "That's too bad. I'll have to call the train company and hope that some nice person has handed it in. It should be alright." Here, your only focus is on the fact that you left the phone on the train, without any anxious thoughts, and subsequently you make this situation feel less troubling to you.

Downplaying how you react towards negative situations is not about sticking your head in the sand, but rather about giving yourself an honest perspective. We frequently react stronger towards negative situations than the situation itself warrants. This is because our reactions are shaped by how we feel at the time. Our reactions get stronger when we are tired, annoyed or stressed. The next time you encounter an everyday problem, try changing the way you react to make it less powerful.

Other common reactions might be: "Leaving my phone on the train – that's just so typically me. I'm such a moron leaving my cellphone like that. I just can't seem to help causing problems for myself." It is not enough that we kick off a long series of anxious thoughts that make us more susceptible to feeling bad, we also increase our sense of frustration significantly through our self-patronizing interpretation of the situation. These kinds of reactions have an extremely negative impact on us, but, unfortunately, they are also very common.

Our reactions influence our subconscious mind, which, in turn, amplifies and programs our future interpretations and feelings. We label ourselves when we make these kinds of generalizations, and in the example above we label ourselves as absent-minded, stupid and that we always create problems. The question is whether this is a fair assessment or if our conclusions are somewhat too dramatic. If you find yourself in a situation where you are condescending towards yourself, stop and try to adopt a larger perspective. Ask yourself if it really is true that you tend to forget things, or if it is just your bad feelings at the moment that create this idea. If you in fact are someone who tends to forget things, then ask yourself if this really makes you a stupid person or someone who is always causing problems.

Our feelings, in other words, are guided by both our thoughts and reactions, but there are of course exceptions. We also have instinctive fears and feelings that manifest themselves so quickly that we do not have time to think. These may appear during times of danger, like if we are attacked by someone or if there is a fire in our house. Apart from these kinds of instinctive feelings, troublesome and difficult feelings often originate in our own thoughts. Imagine taking a run. The first two miles are wonderful. You are enjoying the fresh air, the birds singing and the beauty of nature. But then you start to get tired. What is happening now is that your pleasurable thoughts are starting to get replaced by a completely different set of thoughts: "Man – I can't believe I have three more miles to run. My legs are so heavy. It's difficult even to breathe. I wish I'd be sitting at home right now, in my comfy armchair sipping on a glass of lemonade. Wow, my legs are really starting to cramp up." All of a sudden, your run has been transformed from being pleasurable into pure agony. Another way you could have approached this run would have been to think more along the lines of: "I'm getting a really good workout now. It's going to feel so good when I'm done. I feel strong – I can take this hill – and I have plenty more to give." This would have made you experience completely different feelings than pain and extreme fatigue.

The next time you feel really tired when running, try expressing all the thoughts that make you feel even more tired. Keep reminding yourself that your legs feel really heavy and that you have to quit soon. Remind yourself about all the steep hills ahead of you.

The next time you go out running, after having tried the approach above, instead try to do the complete opposite. Bring forward the kind of thoughts that boost your energy: "I feel so energized today. I feel great! My body feels so light and powerful." It is only when you allow something to become a hardship that it feels like a hardship – until then, it does not have to be hard at all.

Imagine that you are to spend the night in an old abandoned house in the middle of the forest, far away from civilization. You get there in the afternoon. You are thrilled about this and you look forward to getting a good night's rest and to experience the beautiful surroundings. You are reading in front of the open fire and you have a glass of red wine and a bowl of potato chips next to you. You have a wonderful feeling of peace and the surrounding silence gives you a great sense of harmony. Darkness has just enveloped the forest and all of a sudden you hear a strange noise coming from upstairs. Your first thought is: "It's an old house and they tend to make little noises." But you still want to go up to the attic to make sure that you are right. Walking upstairs, you start to notice that the floor is making creaking sounds for every step you take. You can hear the wind starting to pick up outside and the rain pouring down on the building's old windows. The tree branches outside are lightly rubbing up against the walls of the old house and you can now hear tiny noises everywhere. Now, all of a sudden, your mind starts to race: "What if there is something strange about this house and what if someone knocks on the door in the middle of the night? I'm all by myself in the middle of the forest. What if there's someone outside of the building right now?!" Nothing has really happened. You could hear all of these strange noises even in front of the fireplace, but then you did not care and you chose to enjoy the moment. But the much louder sound coming from the attic was the starting point in a chain of anxious thoughts, which, in a matter of minutes, transformed your sense of peace and harmony into fear and horror.

Your sense of peace and harmony was disturbed as your thoughts created fear, but it could just as easily have been disturbed by anxious thoughts about your relationship, your job, your children or your future.

You can exercise your muscles to become more agile, stronger and fit. Scholars say that the brain works the same way. You can exercise your brain to become sharper, faster, more effective and more focused. In just the same way that you can take control over your body, you can also take control over your brain. There are a number of methods for learning how to control your thoughts in order for you to be able to focus all of your attention on the things that really matter in your life.

Look for comfortable feelings

For some strange reason, it is easier for us humans to take notice of the negative instead of the positive.

One way of steering your thoughts towards situations that give you positive feelings is to really look for things that make you happy. When the day is over, you simply summarize what you liked the most during the day. To make this easier, you may prepare a few simple questions about things you feel particularly strongly about, like:

- *What was the most beautiful thing I saw or experienced today?*
- *What was the most fun thing that happened today?*
- *What was the best thing that happened at work or in school?*
- *What was my best moment today?*

If your body often aches, you may ask yourself what felt the best about your body today. If you tend to be tired a lot and lack energy, you may ask yourself when you had the most energy during the day. If you want to increase your self-esteem, you may ask yourself which one of your nice traits you presented the most during the day.

Our brains are built in such a way that it is very difficult for it to think about two things at the same time. Using this simple method, you create more space for thinking about the good things in your life. Focusing on these gives you less space to have negative thoughts.

One day when I was five, I was really, really sad. I remember my mom looking anxiously at me. She sat down in front of me and asked: "What is your absolute favorite thing to do?" In two seconds, I stopped being sad and for the next 15 minutes I told her how much I enjoyed playing soccer. Then I went to fetch my soccer ball and with a big smile on my face I ran down to the neighborhood soccer field. She often made me think about fun things when I was sad, and that made me simply forget why I was sad in the first place. My feelings of sadness were replaced with feelings of joy.

This is something you may consider when you are discussing a pay raise with your boss. Then you may ask: "What do you think are my strengths as a receptionist?" As a salesperson, you may ask your client: "Alright, now I've heard what you think is bad about our company, so why don't you tell me what you like?" Instead of you bringing up the strengths of yourself or your company to the boss, the client or whoever, you get them to tell you about these strengths themselves. The better you get at noticing the good things, the better you will simply become at focusing on the things that have a positive impact on your feelings.

Send out an order

Whatever is important to you at the moment is what you tend to focus your thoughts on. And, when this happens, this is exactly what you will notice. It works sort of like a self-fulfilling prophecy. If we believe that life is fun, we subconsciously tend to seek out situations that give us joy. People expecting a baby often tend to see pregnant women, babies and strollers everywhere. If you are building a sundeck, then you will notice others building sundecks. If you are considering buying the latest Volvo model, then you will all of a sudden notice a lot of people driving this particular car. If you are afflicted with a disease you have never heard of, then you may initially feel like you are the only one suffering from this, but after a while you will start to notice a lot of people suffering from the same disease.

A simple method for attracting "goodies" in your life is to send out an order for what you want. You can send out this order to a higher power or just into the vast expenses of space. You may say: "I wish that I had more luck. I wish that I get a job soon. I wish I bump into a nice person tomorrow." This is an incredibly effective method to actively focus our attention on what we want in life.

"Scaring off"-trigger

A good method for scaring off unwelcome thoughts is that you think of a memory or prepare a thought you really like. This could be a memory from a trip, a funny experience or it could be thinking about someone you like. After that, you create something that triggers this nice thought. When an unwelcome thought demands your attention, you may for instance snap your fingers, which works as an automatic reminder to activate your wonderful thought. What you are doing here, in other words, is creating a trigger that automatically becomes the starting point for the nice thought scaring off the unwelcome one. In this way you keep the gates to your brain closed for unwanted visitors. If you notice that the thought you have prepared is not frightening enough for the unwelcome thoughts, then you need to replace it with something more potent.

The next time you are watching sports on TV, pay attention to just how many kinds of triggers there are in professional sports. They make a fist, they talk to themselves, move a certain way, stroke their cheeks, play with their hair, pull on their clothes, grunt or look at particular things. This is all done to create a wonderful and winning feeling.

Thought tennis

The fact that we have on average 40,000 thoughts each day and that 95% of these are thoughts repeated from yesterday makes it possible to say that we are really good at dwelling on things. It is the process of dwelling on things that makes the thought come to life and makes it grow stronger. With each thought you have, you give birth to a "new life." The more time you spend dwelling on this thought, the more you nourish this "new life." Dwelling on things is something that frequently leads to stress, and psychotherapists say that dwelling on things is the most common cause behind depressions.

Swedish author and psychotherapist Olle Wadström compares dwelling on things to a game of tennis. On one side of the court is the frightening thought and on the other is the calming one. The game begins with the frightening thought serving a ball of anxiety and the calming thought responds with a forehand, which, for the moment, decreases the level of anxiety. However, the calming thought gives

nourishment to the next frightening thought, which quickly strikes back with a vicious backhand. Just like a tennis game where the ball is hit back and forth, the thoughts are flying back and forth and no player seems to want to surrender. An ordinary game of tennis ends after a certain number of sets, but a game of thought tennis may go on for all eternity. It does not end until either the frightening or the calming thought gets tired and surrenders. The best way to end a game of thought tennis is to let the frightening thought win. In this way, you expose yourself to the thing that makes you anxious – which may in the short run raise your level of anxiety – but, in the long run, exposure is the correct antidote to dwelling on things.

It is also possible to find physiological reasons for why we sometimes end up dwelling on things. The reason is that the frightening thoughts create an inner stress, which leads to decreased brain activity. And, if that is not enough, the activity goes down in the very parts of the brain that deal with logical reasoning. This leads to us momentarily giving our brains more space to have primitive and automatic thoughts, which makes it very hard for us to process logical arguments. When we are in this state of mind, it is common that calming thoughts instead tend to create new processes of frightening thoughts. Physiological aspects also clearly indicate that you increase your chances of winning the game of thought tennis if you surrender and stay with the frightening thought for a moment.

A daily moment for thinking

If you frequently have your sense of harmony disturbed by having many different thoughts, then you may devote a moment of every day to do nothing but thinking. When you are under attack from thoughts that you have a hard time letting go, write them down and save them for your daily moment. In order to create a long-term habit of having a daily moment to think, it is helpful to have this moment at the same time every day. How much time you spend thinking depends on how many thoughts you need to process.

The Heart of the Rose

In the Indian Himalayas, there are a number of monks, calling themselves mystics, who live high up in the mountains. They practice an ancient form of meditation called The Heart of the Rose. The purpose is to calm their inner self and to fill it with peace and harmony, while also practicing their ability to control their thoughts. To try this method, I suggest that you sit down comfortably. You put a rose in front of you, and you focus completely on this flower for a few minutes. Look at the rose as intently as you can, and as soon as thoughts not concerning the rose arise, you quickly try to block these and continue to focus on the rose.

If you practice this form of meditation, then you will pretty quickly become good at controlling your thoughts. Regardless of whether you devote two or twenty minutes to The Heart of the Rose, you may let this moment become your daily oasis where you give yourself peace and harmony.

It is possible for you to meditate over other things than just a rose. You may use things like a picture, a beautiful tree, a rock or a cloud. You may also meditate by only focusing on listening to your breathing, to how waves roll in when you are on the beach, how the wind is blowing or how the leaves of the trees are making sounds. When you have used this method every day for a number of weeks, you may also try to focus completely on listening to your family and friends. This method does not only make it possible for you to be able to control your thoughts by sorting out unnecessary things. It also makes you more present, while giving your brain a nice break every day.

As we have previously discussed, the brain has enormous capabilities. In a study, Harvard cardiologist Herbert Benson had some Tibetan monks sit outside wearing nothing but a loin cloth in temperatures below freezing. Then the monks were shrouded in wet blankets. Through meditation, they were able to raise their body temperature to such a degree that they were able to dry the blankets. This experiment was repeated twice and both times the blankets were dry within an hour. It turned out that these monks, by meditating, could raise their body temperature by almost 20°F. They are also able to lower their metabolism by a whopping 60%, which can be compared to the fact that our metabolism only goes down about 15% when we are asleep.

Clouds in the sky

Many of our unwanted thoughts are just like clouds in the sky. They turn up for a short while just to drift away. If you are working on your tan on the beach, you just ignore some clouds. You know that they will simply disappear after a while. But some clouds may be big and dark enough for you to leave the beach. Our thoughts are the same way. Some of them turn up just to disappear shortly after. We do not have to consider these all that much. If you ignore them, they go away. Other thoughts may be very dark and may require some attention before they can go on to drift on by.

Write down disturbing thoughts

By writing down disturbing thoughts, you catch them. This helps you getting structure and it helps you to understand that many of these recurring thoughts are nothing but thoughts you tend to dwell on, thoughts that do not benefit you in any way. Seeing frightening thoughts and thoughts you tend to dwell on written down also makes it easier for you to understand whether or not they are relevant.

"The radio method"

Sometimes we get tired of the constant thought static going around in our brains. Then you may use the so-called "radio method." Pretend that your brain is a radio, find the volume control and turn it down to a more desirable level.

The distraction method

Certainly, you have experienced when you for a short while forget about physical pain, like tooth- or headache? This happens when we momentarily get distracted by something, like being totally caught up in an interesting book, having a deep conversation or when exercising.

It is also possible for you to distract uncomfortable feelings or mental anguish. Let us imagine that you are going to make a toast in front of your whole extended family on Saturday. You may then distract your sense of being nervous by doing something completely different that makes you think about things not at all related to delivering this toast.

If you are experiencing some kind of grief, then you may give yourself a well-deserved break by distracting your feelings of sadness by doing something fun. You may use the distraction method in all kinds of situations that involve any kind of pain or discomfort.

Hire a "brain guard"

Just as we have been taught not to open the front door to unwanted guests, we also need to learn not to open our front door to unwanted thoughts. In many places all around the world, there is even a security guard deciding who will be admitted into

the neighborhood. I have a feeling that the guard who decides which thoughts are allowed entry into your brain has started to get lazy. He lets way too many unwanted thoughts get by him. The question is whether he has fallen asleep on his post or if he has actually abandoned it. My suggestion is that you, starting today, hire a new guard whom you should refer to as the "brain guard." Be clear and tell him that the unwelcome thoughts may be mean and have a very negative impact on you, as well as being thieves stealing your energy and sense of joy. Tell him that the job as a brain guard requires utmost care and that your health and well-being is dependent on how well he performs his task. Tell the brain guard that the unwanted thoughts are so bad that they can even scare off your nice and welcome thoughts.

21
Your inner dialogue

There is an ongoing inner dialogue inside of everyone, and this dialogue gets a different shade depending on our mood. A happy person sees life in brighter shades, where problems and difficulties in fact are terrific opportunities. A depressed person, on the other hand, tends to see life in darker shades, where the opportunities in life are transformed into problems and difficulties.

As soon as the alarm goes off in the morning, thoughts start to buzz around in your head. Each day consists of a constant stream of thoughts. Every thought works as a kind of instruction for your brain. And for every instruction you give your brain, it sends out impulses throughout your body, which in turn affects your mood. A huge number of people have thousands of negative, anxious thoughts each and every day and the vast majority of these people are completely unaware of just how many harmful thoughts they are actually letting into their brain. Some people are very good at keeping out weeds in their gardens, but they are probably not as good at keeping out the "weeds" in the brain.

Having negative and anxious thoughts is something most people accept. They believe that these thoughts are somehow a part of them and that they are simply there to stay. Of course, no thoughts are so set in stone that they are impossible to change, but we need some tools to better be able to change and take control over them. This ongoing stream of thoughts creates an inner dialogue and this dialogue depends on how we feel at a specific moment.

Let us imagine that you start off your day by getting into an early morning fight with your partner. And, since you are both in a hurry to get to work, there is unfortunately no time to settle your dispute then and there. This conflict brings about a series of unpleasant thoughts, which in turn create uncomfortable and annoying feelings. You are driving to work and all of a sudden the car behind you tries to pass you when there is no need whatsoever. Inside of you, the following inner dialogue takes place: "What a moron! I can't believe that there are so many lousy drivers!" You get to work and your boss wants to have a talk with you. Your thoughts continue: "Why can't she just leave me alone? Doesn't she get the fact that I have a lot to do? What a drag..." A client calls you and he is unhappy about something. Your inner dialogue carries on: "Who would have known that all of this garbage would happen on the same day? This hopeless person just ruined my whole day." Your inner dialogue goes on like this all day long.

Now, let us pretend that you are having a nice and cozy breakfast with your partner. You talk about your future, you discuss an upcoming trip and you are having fun together. Later, driving to work, the same car tries to pass you even though there is no need. Your inner dialogue says: "Alright– he's obviously in a hurry." The boss wants to talk to you: "Sure, once again… Well, let's do this, but let's keep it short." The client calls you and he is unhappy. Your inner dialogue carries on: "I actually know what he's saying. We have to fix this. It's a good thing he called so that we can try to solve these issues."

Two identical days and your inner dialogue creates two fundamentally opposite versions. Everything that has a positive impact on how we feel – like sleeping well, a good diet, healthy relationships and avoiding stress – affects our inner dialogue. The scary thing about our thoughts is that we perceive them as true, even though they are nothing but our own interpretations. You could say that they are actually more like some kind of assumptions and guesses.

American psychiatrist and professor emeritus at University of Pennsylvania Aaron Beck developed the so-called cognitive theory in the 1960s. It is frequently said that he has been just as important for the cognitive method as Sigmund Freud was for psychoanalysis. Today we know that anxiety, frustration, despair, depression and anger often originate in distorted thoughts. Using behavioral cognitive therapy, you try to change the patient's thought patterns to create more balance in how the patient perceives himself and his surroundings. Studies show that about 80% of everyone who has suffered from depression will experience this again if they do not change their thought patterns. Cognitive theory has helped countless people and is used all over the world. Aaron Beck has created a universally accepted model for describing our thoughts, and this is based on four different levels.

Core beliefs

These are installed through our childhood experiences and become the very foundation for our identity. They determine how we perceive life, ourselves and those around us. During our first years, these are manufactured through our parents or through others important to us. Our core beliefs are subconscious and we have developed an ability to automatically sort out and adjust information so that it corresponds with our core beliefs. Depending on our childhood experiences, they are positive or negative and are activated through either internal or external stimuli. If, for instance, you have a core belief that you are a wonderful person, then you seek out information confirming this, while turning a blind eye to information indicating the opposite. If, on the other hand, you believe that you are a bad person, then you seek out information supporting this assumption, while ignoring information indicating that you are a good person.

It is only when you become aware of your negative core beliefs that you can discard and change them.

Underlying assumptions

The basis of our underlying assumptions are things like upbringing, cultural/ethnic background, religion, gender, media and the values of our parents and those around us.

Our underlying assumptions determine how we act and how we deal with different kinds of situations. These, in combination with our core beliefs, work as an inner compass, guiding us on the journey through life. Often, our underlying assumptions may prevent us from feeling good, and they frequently prevent us from reaching our full potential as humans.

There are thousands of assumptions, like that one should always be perfect, happy, diligent, honest, funny, high-achieving, social, smart, humble, quiet, bohemian or filling one's life with status. A child who only gets praise when winning, but not when losing, may create an underlying assumption saying: "I'm terrific when I win, but worth nothing when I lose." If a child is only praised when she is good, then there is a risk that she develops an underlying assumption saying: "I only matter when I'm good."

It is frequently the case that our underlying assumptions are the ones crushing our dreams and making us feel good or bad.

Automatic thoughts

Running parallel with our conscious thoughts are the automatic ones, or the "destructive thoughts" as the Dalai Lama refers to them. These are constantly at work and they manifest themselves when we are carrying out our daily tasks, like getting dressed, watching the weather or cooking. They also manifest themselves when we evaluate and interpret certain events and situations. Going back to the reaction about the phone that was left behind on the train, the thought "so typically me" is an automatic thought. These thoughts are treacherous, as they are often subconscious. This means that they go on without any kind of reflection. A lot of people have made being dissatisfied or having critical and negative thoughts into so-called automatic thoughts. These may be activated as soon as we get the slightest feeling that something is boring "Ah, what a drag…" or when we are unlucky "I just never catch a break, do I?" or when driving "Yikes – terrible traffic today" or when someone around us turns out to be somewhat odd "What a bizarre way to act" or in relationships "He never picks up after himself. He never listens to me. She's always whining." There are thousands of automatic thoughts and there are thousands of situations that can trigger them.

Everyone is the sum of their past, and that is why everyone interprets reality in their own way. Depending on our core beliefs and on our underlying assumptions, we perceive reality from different perspectives. Just as the number 6 becomes a 9 when looking at it upside-down. Some kids are only satisfied when they win a soccer game, whereas others are satisfied with a tie. Some teenagers are only satisfied when getting an A+, whereas others are satisfied with a C. Our feelings are often determined by our expectations.

I recently went to see a youth game of soccer. The game ended in a tie and one team was absolutely devastated by this result, while the other team danced around in joy. We constantly perceive life from different perspectives. We all work the same way – both professionally as well as in our personal lives. The same accomplishments, situations and actions lead to different experiences and feelings among different people.

Just as with everything in life, we always have a choice and it is always possible for us to change "the sum of ourselves." When life begins, you could say that we are lying there in our crib with an empty backpack. Just as we fill our backpack throughout life, we may also empty it in order to continue on life's journey with lighter steps. When we dismiss unpleasant thoughts, they end up in our subconscious mind where they all get jumbled together. Thus we fill up our backpack and over time we may find it too heavy to carry. Eventually our body starts to ache and we get anxious and depressed.

Studies show that almost 90% of our 40,000 daily thoughts are negative. This is pretty scary, considering that our negative thoughts are harmful to the brain.

95% of all of your thoughts end up in your subconscious mind. Over time they grow and then they start to work for you. I would say that your subconscious mind gets the right kind of nourishment when you are having positive thoughts and when you sort and work through negative experiences.

Some time ago, I visited a carnival in a medium-sized Swedish town. It was a wonderful night. It was 9 p.m. and the sun was still warm. People were eating, drinking and everyone was in a terrific mood. Pretty soon, Swedish artist Petra Marklund was to go on stage to play some nice music. Everyone was talking to everyone. I found myself talking to a woman in her 60s. When I told her I found this to be a great party, she replied: "Sure, but it's a pity that there aren't more people here." This is an example of an automatic thought. Even though there really was nothing bad about this evening whatsoever, she focused her thoughts on the fact that there were "only" 5,700 people there instead of 6,000.

I recently experienced another example of automatic thoughts. It was a Wednesday night and I was spending the evening with four of my clients at a nice restaurant in Stockholm overlooking the sea. These clients all worked in the same field and we had a lot to talk about. We had a glass of wine and we had a great time. Later it turned out that the waitress had forgotten about our order and, at this moment, a long series of automatic thoughts started to manifest themselves among my clients. Some of them reacted negatively and claimed that the reason why the waitress had forgotten our order was because she did not like us. Someone said that it was a pity we had picked this lousy restaurant and that it felt as if the evening was ruined. But one of my clients decided to look at it in another way and defended the waitress by saying that these things happen, especially on a busy night like this. After a short while he added: "Have you considered how much better the food is going to taste

now that we've waited for so long?" Which one of the four clients do you think enjoyed the rest of the evening the most?

Conscious thoughts

Last, but not least, we also have conscious thoughts. These are used by us when we identify and change automatic thoughts and core beliefs. Through our conscious thoughts, we can create new arguments that guide us. When we try to solve our everyday problems, we usually use our conscious and logical thoughts. These are more balanced and reasoned. They are guided by our will and are based on our intentions and needs.

Thought traps

Swedish motivational speaker Raymond Ahlgren says in one of his lectures that there is a study showing that people on average lie 100-150 times a day. People have a subconscious tendency to spice things up, subtract and adapt what they say to better suit the receiver.

The fact that we believe our thoughts to be true results in us rarely questioning them. What we are actually doing is distorting reality so that it matches our personal truths and underlying assumptions. This can take the form of many different thought traps. Many psychotherapists say that the following are the most common thought traps:

Selective attention – everyone has positive and negative experiences, but what is happening here is that there is a filter leaving out all of the positive. A close friend of mine works as a taxi driver and once related to me this conversation he had with a customer an early spring day:

My friend: "What a lovely day!"
Customer: "I wouldn't know anything about that."
My friend: "Great weather."
Customer: "It's way too hot."
My friend: "But it's lovely listening to all these birds singing."
Customer: "I haven't heard any birds."

Reading my mind – you think that everyone should be able to read your mind, which results in you feeling excluded and misunderstood.

Should and must – you feel, for instance, that you have to get this job, instead of you wanting this job.

A black or white perspective – a small mistake makes you a failure as a person.

Labeling – grading yourself and those around you, while assuming that your assessments are objective facts.

Magnifying and shrinking – mistakes are magnified and accomplishments shrunk in size.

Fortune telling – foreseeing all kinds of negative situations in the future.

Thoughts of catastrophes – you believe that the worst will happen.

Generalization – a prior negative experience creates an inner belief, which in turn creates preconceived notions like: "It will never work. It's always the same with her. All men are like that."

So, in conclusion, our thoughts often provide us with information that does not entirely correspond with reality. When we become aware of our core beliefs and our automatic thoughts, we make it possible for us to change them. Feeling good often happens when life is in balance and this, in turn, affects our inner dialogue.

22
Helping thoughts

The same thought may give you wings or may lead you into complete darkness. Your thoughts are extremely powerful and a small tweak in the wording of a thought may be enough to determine whether the same thought makes you fly or crash.

People constantly push themselves to the sidelines in order to focus on their work, family, friends and everything that needs to be done in their everyday lives. We often feel that we need more alone time, but we rarely make sure that we give ourselves the time we really need. We believe that there are always things that need to get done, that there is a lot to do at work or that our family needs us. That is how it is – your family and work need you and you are always busy trying to make everything fall into place. This is exactly why you need to give yourself the necessary amount of time, so that you can give those around you nothing but the best from you. Consider what you need for yourself, what makes you feel really good, what makes you the best parent possible or what makes you a really good person. Give yourself what you need because you care about yourself and those around you.

Having the right thought patterns will reduce all of life's demands and create more space for all the good things in life. Let us look at how your thoughts may easily assist you in your everyday life.

You are good just the way you are

We should be giving ourselves the very best in order to become the best, but instead we make ourselves feel guilty about not doing this or the other. We ought to spend more time with our children, see our friends more often, fix up the house, meet our parents, exercise, clean up and put away money for our retirement. When it

is possible for us to relax, guilt kicks in. Our thoughts buzz around: "There's so much I need to do, but look at me. Just sitting around." A lot of people create this subconscious notion that they, for some reason, are not as good a person just because they are relaxing and doing nothing. Instead of feeling lazy for not doing anything, we should enjoy these moments and be proud that we give ourselves time to relax. When we are just kicking back, we are in fact investing in our own health – something that will benefit everyone around us.

Unfortunately, we make ourselves feel guilty for no good reason at all. Why is that? No one feels better just because you feel guilty. The only result is that you feel worse. If you feel worse, you will become a worse parent. You will probably take more energy from those around you and you will surely perform worse at work. You are good just the way you are and you deserve to feel good. There are a myriad of things you need to do to make your life work, but nothing is more important than you feeling good. Allow yourself to be flawed. Allow yourself to not be perfect. Allow yourself to simply be human. Allow yourself to feel that you are good just the way you are!

Replace feelings that are hard to come by

It is Friday and the last day of the week. We should be enjoying the fact that we get to go home soon and that we do not have to work for an entire weekend. But what do we do instead? We get stressed and maybe also annoyed because the desk will not be "clean" by the time we go home. So what if there are things left for us to do come Monday? When you find yourself in this situation, consider the consequences of your tasks being unfinished until next week. Maybe you can prioritize Friday's work so that you save the least important things for the afternoon, and if you notice that you will not have the time to finish them towards the end of the day, then it is surely no problem dealing with these less important tasks next week.

Frequently, what is really at stake here is not finishing the last tasks of the week, but rather that we want to feel as if this week's tasks are all finished when we leave on Friday. The next time you feel stressed about not having enough time to finish everything you want to before the weekend, stop and try to get rid of the need to have a feeling of being done. Instead, focus on the feeling of being off work. In this way, you replace a feeling that is often hard to come by with another nice feeling, which is much more accessible.

Throughout life, we create situations that lead to both pleasant and unpleasant feelings. We easily get used to situations that create these nice and pleasant feelings. Sometimes, though, we may be in a phase in our lives where we are no longer capable of putting ourselves in the kind of situations that generate these great feelings. It is, however, always possible for us to change our own behavior, or our habits, so that we may get rid of our need to be in a specific situation to get a certain feeling. We can learn to replace one nice feeling with another. If, for instance, we exercise regularly and this makes us feel good, then it is easy to come to the conclusion that we would feel worse if we got injured and were unable to exercise. But things do not have to be this way. We could actually feel just as good as when we are exercising. We simply need to replace the feeling we get from exercising with another enjoyable feeling. This could be something like a new hobby, a new friend, a new project or focusing on fulfilling a dream.

Some people hit a bump in life when they retire. This is often due to the fact that they have lost the habit of going to work. But, as we know, there are loads of things that may replace this feeling. We can meet new friends, get new hobbies, go on picnics, read, do charity work and travel. What many people who like shopping have in common, for instance, is that it is the very act of shopping itself that creates a feeling. Frequently, it is not really about actually needing a new pair of shoes, even though they may tell themselves that. It is the act of buying the shoes that creates a nice feeling. Shopping itself does not necessarily have to be a problem, but you should obviously try to break the need to shop if this is causing you financial problems. What you need to do then is to find something to replace the feeling you get when shopping. The brain is built in such a way that it releases different kinds of neurotransmitters, like endorphins and dopamine, when we do things we enjoy. This is exactly what happens when we exercise, travel, spend time with friends, laugh or shop. What this means is that the feeling you get when shopping is not connected to shopping as such. It is connected to the fact that you simply like doing things you enjoy. This means that you may replace the feeling you get from shopping with something else you know you enjoy, like nature walks, music, meeting friends, etc.

Inspiring words

Simply rephrasing a thought may inspire us instead of holding us back. We have a great number of thought patterns creating pressure, stress and anxiety.

Most of the time, it is not the everyday life itself making us stressed, but the way we think about it. The pressure does not necessarily have to come about by *what* we think, but from *how* we think. Let me explain. You wake up Monday morning and think: "Now I *have* to go to work." The next time you are leaving for work, instead try to think: "Now I *want* to go to work." Surely, it sounds much nicer thinking: "I *want* to work. I *want* to exercise. I *want* to paint my house." Another way of thinking would be: "I *choose* to go to work in order to get paid."

Thoughts like *must, should, have* to and *shall* create a process inside of us that creates an inner pressure. These kinds of phrases produce a feeling of demands and musts. Thoughts like *want* to, *wish* and *choose*, on the other hand, create a sense of anticipation, which in turn gives us a sense of freedom. In this way, we create a feeling that we actually have a choice. You can always use this kind of rephrasing. In sports, you may switch out the thought pattern of I *have* to win to I *want* to win. In your relationship, you may switch from I *have* to be a good boyfriend to I *want* to be a good boyfriend. About you as a person, you may change your approach from I *have* to become a better person to I *want* to become a better person. Consider whether there is a situation where you believe that you have to do something, where it would instead be possible for you to think that you *want* to do it. Every day we need to motivate ourselves to go to work and do all the things we have to do. The better you get at motivating yourself, the more you will enjoy life.

You seldom get motivated to do something when you are forced to do it. Most of the time, the greatest inspiration comes about when you actually want to do something. Consider what it would mean to you and your life if your inner drive got stronger. Also consider your thought patterns. Is it possible for you to change some words in order to get more motivated and get more drive?

Maximize yourself

No matter how hard we work to increase our inner drive, there will always be days when it is hard to find any kind of inspiration. A common scenario is that we wake up in the morning, feeling tired and like we are running a cold. We rush off to work. We get to work with absolutely no energy whatsoever and all we want to do is to go home and go back to sleep. Or maybe we feel guilty and annoyed that we are unable to perform as well as we normally do.

When we feel completely under the weather, we first and foremost need to accept the fact that we are having a bad day. If our capacity is not at 100% today, then what is it? 50%? 70%? Let us say that on this particular day, your capacity is at 50%. Then you need to figure out how you are going to get the most out of these 50%. Believing that you will accomplish more than you feel that you can handle today is unrealistic. But if you manage to reach today's maximum capacity of 50%, then you know that you have done the absolute best you can. This means that you can be satisfied with yourself when you go home at night. You performed as well as you could. Your capacity was at 50% and you reached it, which is a 100% accomplishment.

Focus on the whole picture

Some days it is hard to finish everything we need to do. Even when we choose not to do some things, there is simply not enough time. During these days, we need to accept that we will not be able to do everything we should. On days when we struggle to find the time, we need to accept that it is in fact OK if some things do not turn out perfectly. Some time ago, I felt enormously stressed about everything I needed to get done during the week. Discussing this with a colleague, he asked me: "Is it necessary that you complete all of your tasks perfectly? Isn't it enough that the larger end result is as good as possible?"

We frequently focus too much on specific things, and if we do a mediocre job with these, then we get disappointed. But, surely, isn't what matters in the end the whole picture and not the smaller pieces?

Motivate yourself

Let us pretend that you are at work on a Thursday afternoon. You feel tired and you want to go home and chill out. It is 3 p.m. and you get off in two hours. You have more or less finished what you needed to get done today and you find it hard to motivate yourself to work. What do you do? Maybe you look at your watch 15 minutes later and conclude that time surely goes by slowly. In the morning, it is easier for us not to think about the time. Why is that? Why do so many of us get so fixated on the time in the afternoon – something that in itself makes the time go by much slower?

It is obvious that we know in the morning that there is still much left of the day, and this makes it easier for us to focus on the tasks at hand instead of focusing on the time and on going home. This makes the time go by faster. If you throughout your day find yourself lacking motivation and instead start looking at your watch, ask yourself what you need at that very moment to get motivated. Try creating an environment where you give yourself the motivation you need to enjoy work and, therefore, get the most out of your day. Sometimes all it takes is a tiny change to increase your motivation. It could be something like having an afternoon coffee break with your colleagues or saving the most enjoyable tasks for the afternoon.

Thank yourself for your mistakes

There is only one kind of person who goes through life without making any mistakes and that is someone who goes through life without living.

Mistakes are the most valuable investments we can make in our personal growth. We make a lot of mistakes because we simply have not learned how to do those things yet. Do you remember making mistakes all the time when you were a kid? When you learned how to speak, things often turned out wrong. When you learned how to walk, you tripped and when you learned how to eat, you made a huge mess. You made thousands of mistakes, but because of them you also learned hundreds of new things. Thank yourself for your mistakes instead of letting them annoy you.

Focus on the end result

No matter how much we struggle to create thought patterns that motivate us, it is unavoidable that some things may seem horrendously boring. Let us imagine that you are about to clean your home. You are looking around your apartment. You notice all the dust and grime, and you know how much work you have ahead of you. Cleaning feels more and more like a hardship. Do you recognize yourself here? When we see all of the dust and all of the work we have to do, things feel more difficult to us. How do we get rid of this difficult feeling?

We may focus our thoughts on the end result of having a clean home. We may focus our thoughts on how nice it will look once we are done. We may visualize how our newly cleaned apartment looks and how nice it smells. A lot of us use the same method when dealing with possible difficult feelings before going to the gym for example. We instead focus on the wonderful feeling we get after a great workout.

23
Limiting identities

In today's society, we tend to build our identity on things like our profession. Maybe you identify with being an accountant, an entrepreneur or a receptionist. You have a sense of pride in this identity – which is all good – but what happens when you fail in your professional role?

Experts worldwide agree that men feel significantly worse than women when they retire. The reason is that they identify so strongly with their profession. Women, on the other hand, do not identify as strongly with their work. They tend to have other things in their lives they value higher. Some men who retire get a feeling that they are losing themselves, and some even come to think that their value as a person diminishes somewhat.

Some people about to move say: "It's going to be wonderful moving to this new place. No one knows who I am there and I get to be whoever I want to be." Who says you cannot be exactly who you want to be right here and now?

Everyone identifies with something. How you perceive yourself is crucial for how your life will evolve. Some people identify with always being happy, others with being ambitious. But what happens when this person no longer has the energy to be happy or ambitious? There are thousands of things we can identify with. I have an acquaintance who identifies with always having bad luck. As far as I can tell, she is no more lucky or unlucky than anyone else. The problem is that she always thinks that she is unlucky and as soon as she is, she is very quick to point out just how unlucky she is. When things go her way, however, she does not seem to take notice.

It is also common to identify with a life situation, like being a widow, an addict, disabled, unemployed or poor. Be that as it may, but we are so much more than just that. At the same time as being unemployed, for instance, you may also be a parent, a sister, a good friend, a good daughter plus hundreds of other things. Why, in that case, do you have to label yourself unemployed?

Most athletes have something in common. They identify strongly with their role as an athlete and as a competitive person. When Swedish high jumper Stefan Holm was still active, he once said: "I can't imagine who I am if I can't be that high jumper. Who am I now is what I would ask myself." So, what really happens when an athlete fails in a competition? The risk is that this person sees himself as a failure, instead of realizing that he is an athlete who simply failed in a single competition. Many people react the exact same way when they do not succeed with a task at work. For some people, a single mistake at work may have a severe effect on their lives. The reason is that they feel like failures, instead of considering the fact that all they did was to fail in one particular instance at work. Just the same way the professional athlete needs to separate her role as an athlete and as a person, we need to separate our professional roles from our role as a person. The mere fact that we fail in one particular field does not make us a less valuable person. We were just not as good in this particular field at this particular time.

What do you identify with? Consider whether how you identify yourself is fair or whether you are more than "just" that. Consider whether the way you identify yourself may constrain you or hold you back in life.

The reason why it is so important to consider this is because we label ourselves based on what we identify ourselves with. This label will affect us. The unfortunate one says: "Bad luck as usual" and the fortunate one says: "I knew things would work out." The unemployed one says: "It surely is tough being on the outskirts of society," whereas the one who sees himself as lucky will say: "Life sure is great." Depending on how we label ourselves, we create limitations and possibilities. We need to become aware of how this affects us. Sure, it could be that those around you are the ones labeling you, but you are the one who decides whether to let the label stick or not. What this means is that you yourself have the power to decide whether or not to live your life according to the label assigned to you by others.

Just because you work in a certain profession, have a certain history or have been the same way all your life does not mean that you are not allowed to or cannot change what you identify with. We are so much more than what we do, what we have done and what we accomplish. First and foremost, we are all humans and we are all equally precious.

You are free to be whoever you want to be. Consider who and how you want to be, and then start to be that person.

24
Live your dreams

Walt Disney once said: "If you can dream it, you can do it." Everything you see around you originates in a dream. Thomas Alva Edison invented the light bulb. He failed countless times, but his dream was so strong that he never gave up. If you are sufficiently motivated, I would argue that you can make any dream come true.

There is no universal way for achieving your particular dream, but one crucial factor is that you have the right drive. Observing people who have made their dream come true, while becoming happier by doing so, we can notice that they have had change, improvement, self-realization or growth as their driving force. It is also clear that those who have had money, status or fame as their motivation do not get happier once they achieve their dream. These kinds of driving forces are nothing but temporary and only make you happy for the moment.

Why is it that so many beautiful dreams never come true? I would say that it is because of two things. First, we are not sufficiently mentally prepared, which increases the risk that we give up along the way. Second, we do not even try to make the dream come true. Maybe you recognize excuses like: "I simply don't have the time. I'm too old. I can't afford it. I don't want to make myself disappointed. I'm simply not the right guy. I wouldn't be able to anyway." People are experts at finding excuses for not realizing their dreams.

That we refrain from trying is often because we do not take the dream seriously. We believe that it is nothing but a dream. It could also be because we lack the know-how for realizing a particular dream. Or it could be that we do not have enough faith in ourselves to work up the courage to take that first step. If we are certain that we will make our dream come true, then we will most certainly try to make this happen.

Far too many people reluctantly go to work each morning. Every once in a while they perhaps start thinking about going back to school or having the courage to apply for that other job they have considered for so long. But for many people it ends in a dream and life goes on as usual. Realizing the dream in most cases means a certain degree of change, which is scary for many people.

Another very common kind of behavior is that we love to dream in general. We dream about that designer house, travelling the world in a sailing boat, writing a novel, changing careers, living in Antarctica or taking singing lessons. On the other hand, our current life is working out just fine and we feel more or less satisfied. We do not consider that we can actually make most of our dreams come true. We also do not consider what it would really mean to us and our lives if we actually realized this dream.

When we were kids, we dared being more open in our minds. We were less self-conscious, which helped us dream more freely about the future. Later on, we became more influenced by the expectations of those around us and by notions about how things should be. Throughout life, we create more boundaries for what we think is right for our life. The older we get, the more difficult it is for us to dream without any restrictions, as we are influenced by all of these external factors. As adults, we tend to be more realistic and we have a tendency to consider the most practical thing for us to do. We take whole sets of aspects into consideration, which tends to limit us greatly. This, in turn, makes it harder for us to live our lives to the fullest.

As a child, you were much less limited in your thoughts and dreams. What did you dream about then? Consider whether any of your childhood dreams still tickle your imagination today. Maybe you wanted to be an officer of the law, live in the deepest of the jungles of Africa together with all the animals or, perhaps, you had the same dream I had – namely to become the number one in the world in table tennis, tennis and soccer at the same time, and preferably before I was 18, when my goal was to become a happy businessman. Being the world champion in three sports at the same time did not strike me as odd. Perhaps this dream was not all that realistic, but it gave me inspiration and this dream made me happy. Because that is how a lot of our dreams work. They give us hope, inspiration and joy, but unfortunately we also lose way too many important dreams. Even though a particular dream may be very strong and realistic, we may nevertheless put it aside just to eventually forget all about it. Some dreams are difficult to recover, but if we find them again, then they would be just as strong today.

We may choose to deny other dreams. Sometimes there is something inside of us making us push certain dreams away, but it is very likely that once again, later in life, they resurface. We hear older people saying things like: "Why didn't I put more effort into my career? Why didn't I travel more? Why didn't I climb that mountain? Why didn't I learn more languages? Why didn't I simply enjoy life more?" In order for you to not let your most precious dreams go to waste, I suggest that you go through the following exercise:

1. Write down all of your dreams

Write down the dreams you had as a child, as a teenager and the dreams you have today. Have a completely open mind and do not consider whether your dreams are realistic or not. Consider what lights up that spark inside of you. Do you have a true passion? Is it at all possible to turn your passion into your livelihood? If it turns out that you lack a passion in your life, then your dream could be to go out and explore what really lights up that fire inside of you. Remember that it is never too late to create a new life passion.

Do you have dreams you have postponed or do you perhaps have a dream you for some reason have avoided or repressed?

2. Now pick your three most powerful dreams

Take your time. Fantasize what your life would be like if one of your dreams came true. Imagine how this would make you feel and how it would affect you as a person.

3. Consider whether these dreams are truly your *own*.

Sometimes dreams are instilled in us through those around us. Perhaps your parents had well-meaning visions for your future life and later these visions transform into your dreams. Have you recently considered why you are actually working or studying in your present field?

Some time ago, I was having a conversation with two businesswomen. They were old childhood friends and they had always been around one another. I asked them why they work in the field of business. One of them answered that she had always found business very interesting, so for her the choice was simple. The other woman answered that she had been very keen to study together with her friend, and that is why she had picked the same business program. When she was younger, she dreamt of working as a teacher or as a psychologist. But today she works in the business world due to the fact that she 15 years earlier wanted to study together with her best friend. This is a world she actually does not care for.

Another time, I found myself talking to a woman who worked in a kindergarten. She told me that growing up she had constantly been told that she was very good with children. This lead to her starting to work in a kindergarten. Today, 25 years later, she told me that she had always found this job extremely tough and she had been thinking about quitting for quite some time. She also told me that she had never really been all that interested in working with children.

Realizing a dream while, at the same time, being happy for having done so could be construed as impossible if you do not long for this dream at the bottom of your heart. Be very careful that your dreams really are your own dreams. I would venture to promise you that if you have a strong inner drive to make this dream come true, then it is your very own dream.

4. Consider what you are ready to sacrifice for your dream

Swedish professional athlete Susanna Kallur once said: "I am trading my life for what I want to accomplish, and my injuries are the price for this dream." This may seem like a huge sacrifice. Consider what you are willing to give up. How much time, energy and money are you willing to give up and what kind of sacrifices are you willing to make in order to make your dream come true? Then ask yourself if it is worth it. If the answer is yes, then your inner drive is probably strong enough for you to realize this dream.

5. Make a list of your dreams and focus on one of them

Which one of the three dreams you picked is the most important to you right now? Which one of these dreams would be suitable to realize depending on where you are in life at the moment? Ask yourself why this particular dream is so important to you. Then focus all of your thoughts on this particular dream. You increase your chances of reaching your dream if you focus on one dream at a time.

6. Write down the advantages of realizing this dream

If, for instance, you want to get another job, then possible advantages could be new colleagues, inspiration, personal growth, higher salary, freedom, change or less stress.

7. Now look at the list of advantages

Surely it is worth your while going for this dream?

8. Transform the dream into a set of intermediate goals

In order to make your dream more tangible and attainable, you need to break it down into smaller intermediate goals. If your dream is to start your own business, then a smaller goal could be to create a good business idea. Another goal could be to get the know-how required to run a business. Getting the necessary financing to implement your business idea could be the next intermediate goal.

9. Create an action plan

Now you need to consider the nuts and bolts for realizing your dream. Look at your intermediate goals and create your action plan accordingly.

10. Create a time limit for your dream

You should no longer postpone this dream. And you will not be able to procrastinate if you give yourself a deadline. Also put up deadlines for your intermediate goals.

11. Prepare those around you

Tell your friends and family that you need to dedicate a lot of time towards this dream and that you will need their support. Also tell them how you are feeling now that you are about to take that one first step towards realizing your dream. If something frightens you, tell them. The more you let those around you understand how you feel, the more supportive they will be.

12. Create a setting that gives you inspiration

You need to constantly provide yourself with the energy required to fulfill your dream. You may do so by spending time in settings where you meet likeminded people. Maybe you can connect with someone who has already made a similar dream come true. That could give you valuable guidance and good advice.

I would say that your chances of realizing your dream are now very good indeed. You have identified the dream you want to realize at this stage in your life and you have come to understand what it would mean to you to make this dream come true. You have broken the dream down into a set of smaller intermediate goals and you have created an action plan. You have also given yourself deadlines. For all intents and purposes, there is nothing holding you back on your journey towards your dream, but first you need to go through a couple of steps to prepare yourself mentally:

1. Have the courage to believe in your dream

Keep telling yourself that you are the right person to fulfill this particular dream. If you remind yourself frequently enough, you will eventually be convinced deep down.

2. Disassemble various kinds of mental obstacles

What mostly makes us quit or not even try are our own mental obstacles. But I know that you can disassemble them through your thoughts. Imagine driving in your car. All of a sudden you come to a road that is completely snowed over and impossible to pass. If, however, a plow truck were to drive ahead of you, then you could easily continue on your drive. A lot of our mental obstacles are connected to our fears and just like the plow truck removing snow from the road, you may also remove mental obstacles with your thoughts so that you can make your dream come true.

3. Create a mental image of success

Close your eyes for a minute. Imagine the feeling running through your body when you finally realize your dream. As we have discussed above, some parts of the brain have a hard time separating imagined from real situations. What this means is that if you fantasize and consider how you are to realize your dream, the brain receives signals that the dream has already come true. This feeling will come in handy on the journey towards your dream.

However, you need to be prepared for encountering skepticism from those around you. People you know may say things like "it can't be done" or "that seems tricky." But remember that everyone lives according to different kinds of truths and in their world it may indeed seem tricky (see chapter 4). That does not necessarily mean that it will be tricky for you.

You may also encounter skepticism originating from yourself. It is often easier for us to resist the skepticism from those around us. The biggest threat is usually found within ourselves. When we try to make a dream come true, it is almost inevitable that we have doubts. Common thoughts are: "What if I fail? This is a mistake. Am I really the right one to do this? What have I gotten myself into?" This is a critical phase and it is very easy to quit at this point. If, however, you have a mental image of success you can summon, then you will be reminded of your inner strength and of the great feeling you will get to experience once your dream comes true.

4. Remember to enjoy the journey towards your dream

We dream of realizing this particular dream, but once we are right in the middle of it, we tend to change it into instead dreaming of having completed it. Maybe you dream of building your own house. But when you are right in the middle of doing so, chances are that you will start to look forward to having completed your house. Once the house is finished, maybe you start dreaming about the cozy garden, patio or swimming pool, and once you are living these dreams, you will think: "As soon as this is all done, then everything will be just fine and dandy." So, instead of enjoying being a part of your big dream, you wish for it to be over. Isn't the point of a dream to enjoy it? Because constantly looking forward to things to come is sort of like dreaming that life should be over as soon as possible.

People who make their dreams come true tend to love doing exactly what they are doing. If we focus too much on the outcome of the dream, it becomes harder to really concentrate on it or enjoying the actual realization of the dream. It is on the road towards the dream that we get to have the biggest experience, because that is when it happens. The feeling of being right in the middle of the journey towards the dream is usually described as both satisfying and powerful. Frequently, this feeling is so great that things we normally perceive as negative and difficult tend to fade in the bright light of the dream. A powerful dream takes up such a large part of our inner self that there is simply no room for negative thoughts.

You could say that people have three inner voices: the dreamer who dreams about the future and of change, the realist who says what is actually possible and the coward who issues warnings. It is the coward who often ends up stopping us when we want to make our dreams come true. Your inner dreamer tells you: "I want to sail around the world." The realist says: "Then I need to take a lot of time off work, and how am I to manage that financially?" The coward, finally, says: "I could never do that. It's way too dangerous. And I am actually not that good at sailing." Depending on who you are, you tend to listen more or less to one of your three inner voices. We need to learn to find a balance between the dreamer, the realist and the coward. All of these three voices have their own role to play, but we need to listen to them in a good way.

The realist reminds you that you need to plan for your financial situation and to have a plan for how you are going to manage to have that much time off. Having a plan may be sufficient for the realist to calm down. I see the coward as the biggest threat for why you do not even start trying to realize certain dreams. We need to give the coward a sense of safety and we may do this by arguing in the following way: "At this moment in time, I may not be able to sail around the world, but if I take lessons in sailing and prepare myself as well as I can, then I will be able to do it." Do not let your cowardly inner voice scare you. Listen to it and use the voice as good advice ahead of a great challenge.

Sometimes we judge ourselves harshly because some dreams never came true, but we must not forget about all the things we have actually accomplished. Remember that where you are today is a result of everything you have accomplished so far. Have the courage to dream about your future. Have the courage to listen to your dreams and to change your life, so that you may live in your dreams.

When you make your dreams come true, you grow as a person and you are presented with new opportunities. You give your heart joy, which in turn rubs off on those around you. Also remember that the fact that you have realized your dream also inspires those around you to do the same. So, by making your dreams come true, you also plant the seeds for the dreams of the people you know.

I know that there is a lot that can hold you back from trying to fulfill a dream, but then start by just taking one tiny step – the first step.

25
Live now

When you are completely present in the moment, you create a space for spontaneous and pleasant feelings. Your presence also intensifies your feelings.

Have you ever forgotten what you said in a conversation? Then you can be really satisfied with yourself, as you have then been 100% present. When we hear a star athlete saying, after some great feat, that he does not remember anything, then we know that this person was completely present. At the same time, some people are so absent that they become spectators to their own lives.

Jonathan Swift once said: "Very few people live for today, most people make preparations for tomorrow." Most people are going somewhere and there are only a few who live in the here and now. Consider what it would mean to your life if you were to learn how to live more in the present.

The brain has a really annoying habit, and that is that it automatically wants to meddle in things. Think back to a situation when you performed at the top of your ability or when you were really happy. What made you perform so well and what made you feel so good? Of course, it is not completely random why you feel happier some days compared with others. It is also not random when you perform at the top of your ability at your job or in sports. These are the days when you are most likely completely present.

Someone once said: "We learn different tools and then we learn to use them. Then we learn to forget them while using them." If, for instance, you want to learn how to tango, you first need to learn the different basic steps, and then how to use them while dancing. Once you have practiced long enough, you will stop thinking about how to use these different steps. Everything you have learned is now in your muscle memory and you are able to do it without thinking. This is when you dance your absolute best.

An average golfer may play extraordinarily well for a few holes. As we always want to play this good, there is a risk that we start thinking: "Why am I this good today? What is special about this day?" All of a sudden we lose our presence and instead we become aware of our great game. At this very moment, we cease to be great. The brain has meddled and ruined our fantastic round of golf.

Let me explain why the brain so frequently ruins things when it interferes. When we do something a number of times, a muscle memory is created. This memory works best when left to do its thing automatically. If, during a round of golf, you start to worry about your strikes or about your technique, then signals are created in the brain that interfere with the parts of the brain that know how to hit the ball the best way. This is how our brains work no matter what we do. Try doing something as basic as talking, walking or typing while you try to figure out how you actually do these things. My guess is that it does not feel as natural as earlier. Just as we exercise our muscle memory to work automatically when performing these everyday tasks, our muscle memory needs to work automatically when we want to perform well in all kinds of contexts.

Meanwhile, you need to find that crucial balance. If everything we do is automatic, then we will not get to grow all that much. If, for instance, we look at your learning curve for driving, my guess is that it went up rapidly in the beginning and then started to decrease. Today, you drive more or less completely automatically, which also means that you have not grown all that much as a driver. Consider athletes – they are very aware of their technique during practice. They analyze what does not feel good about certain strokes and movements and they try to find solutions for how to improve. This is also one of the reasons why top athletes rarely perform at their very best during practice. During a competition, however, they mostly limit their thoughts to the weaknesses of their opponents. They focus on how to best use these weaknesses to their advantage.

Professional athletes have taught themselves to shut off their brain during competitions and to act completely automatically based on their muscle memory. They have taught themselves to let their muscle memory work without interference from the brain. When a hockey player starts to consider his technique and how he moves in the middle of a game, then this is often an indication that he has not practiced enough. Doing sports, we perform our very best when we manage to forget about ourselves and when we simply perform automatically based on our muscle memory.

We work exactly the same way in our everyday lives, at work, as parents, as friends and as family members. We often get the most out of ourselves and perform better when we manage to shut off the brain and let the muscle memory do its thing.

When you are present, you give your senses more room to absorb all of the external inputs. If your mind is drifting away when you are standing on a cliff looking out across the ocean, then it is more or less impossible for you to enjoy the moment to the fullest. Your thoughts are blocking the energy flow in your five senses and the way they interact. If, on the other hand, you manage to gather your thoughts and to only focus on this very moment, a free flow for your senses is created. While watching the beautiful horizon, you pick up the wonderful smells of the ocean. You can hear the waves breaking against the rugged cliffs below and you can feel the warm rays of the sun against your skin - all the while tasting the sweet life.

The more we practice letting the brain's muscle memory work undisturbed, the more effective it will become. At the gym we exercise our physical muscles, and by using our thoughts and other exercises we practice our muscle memory. At the gym we need to exercise regularly to keep and develop our muscles. Our brains work the same way. We need to constantly develop and strengthen the different functions in the brain. But, no matter how much we try to become completely present, we are constantly challenged by different kinds of distractions. In order to deal with these distractions, we need to learn how to quickly recognize the most common traps when trying to be present.

Worrying about the future

It is very hard to be present while thinking about what you are going to do later. While having coffee with a friend, it is all too easy to let your mind drift off and start thinking about something you are going to do later in the afternoon. At the same time as you are having coffee with your friend, you start to think about what to get at the grocery store on your way home or perhaps you are trying to figure out how to solve some problem at work. Isn't it strange that we set aside time to have coffee with a friend, but when we are doing just that, we think about what to do afterwards? Life is happening at this very moment, but in our mind we often choose to be somewhere completely different. But sometimes it could be that we have some kind of inner anxiety that makes it hard for us to be present in the moment: "What if I miss my train? What if I lose my job? What if I can't pay my bills? What if my relationship turns sour?"

Worrying about the future is extremely common, but surely isn't it often the case that the things you worry about never materialize? Instead, you encounter loads of other kinds of problems you never prepared yourself for. Worrying about things that have not yet happened is sort of like paying off loans you do not have. There is no way you can predict all the problems and obstacles you will face in life. Instead, focus your thoughts on what you really can influence, which is this moment right here and now.

Worrying about the past

We easily tend to get stuck in thoughts about past events like: "Too bad I didn't succeed yesterday. Too bad she got so angry. We were so unlucky. What if I had had the courage to take my life in another direction?" These are things you cannot change – they are thoughts that do nothing but disturb your present sense of harmony. I know that it is difficult, but try not to let what happened yesterday hold you back today. Every day is like a new life. What happened yesterday really does not matter. Today is a brand new day, and you decide for yourself how this day will evolve. This is when life is happening and it is right now that you can influence your future.

Acceptance

When you accept the fact that the future is hard to control, and that the past is lost moments, it becomes easier for you to live in the reality that surrounds you at this very moment.

Look for one good trait in everyone you meet

Other people's personality traits may easily disturb our sense of being present. We may get annoyed by someone who talks too much or who is a bad listener.

If, on the contrary, we were to teach ourselves not to focus on the negative aspects of this person and instead focus on the positive ones, then I promise you that you will get much more out of this moment. One method for not getting annoyed by people's flaws is to instead focus on one good trait in everyone you meet. When focusing on trying to find that one good trait, you make it more difficult to subconsciously focus on what is bothering you. When we think about the negative aspects of others, we create a feeling of being annoyed and this disturbs our inner sense of harmony. Conversely, we create a nice feeling when we consider the positive sides of people. The next time you find yourself in a situation where you start to get annoyed by something about the person you are talking to, stop yourself at once. Ask yourself if keeping on having this negative thought benefits you in any way. If the answer is no, then start looking for positive aspects about this person.

Judging and evaluating

In order to help us make decisions, the brain is set up to make different kinds of assessments and judgment calls. This is why it is so immensely difficult to be in different places or among people without starting to evaluate things. We automatically tend to evaluate what others are saying, and if we, for example, find ourselves in a beautiful spot, then we may start to evaluate and judge all kinds of things: "Why did they put that bench there? That tree certainly is beautiful. It looks pretty weird over there. It seems lonely living like this. That plant is just so ugly. It smells so good here." Because we are so focused on judging things, we tend to miss out on the actual experience.

The next time you are spending time with a friend or at a beautiful location, try to simply observe and feel what you see, hear and experience, without passing judgment or evaluating. Only focus on picking up tastes and smells without trying to ascertain whether they are good or bad – just feel them.

The need to be acknowledged

A lot of people have a strong need to be loved by everyone. People who focus on pleasing those around them have a harder time being present in the moment. Instead of focusing on the here and now, and to be totally present in the conversation, this person focuses on being liked. He tends to focus his thoughts on how others perceive him and what they think about his behavior. Let me comfort you by saying that those closest to you love you, and if there are people who do not like you, then that is not your problem. It is their problem. Consider what you really value the most. That a colleague finds you happy and nice to be around, or if you feel happy and have a nice time? If you focus on how you are perceived and strive to make a good impression on everyone you meet, then there is a great risk that you lose your sense of being present. Instead assume that everyone you spend time with likes you.

Having "what-am-I-going-to-say-now" thoughts

Some people have a hard time simply staying quiet and listening. These individuals are usually considering what to say next. They focus on finding a good opportunity for joining the conversation in order to say their piece. It is more or less impossible for this kind of person to be present in a conversation. But consider that when you talk, you teach others, but when others talk, you are the one being taught. Really learning how to listen opens up a brand new world of valuable knowledge, joy and new ideas. To really listen is about being given a glimpse of someone else's life and life history. The more curious you are, the easier it is for you to listen. If you feel that your level of interest is decreasing, change the subject by asking a few questions.

Focus on what you do and not who you are

A lot of people tend to mix up what they do with what they are. A few years ago, I was told about how a group of people dealt with the results of an IQ test. Ten of these people had scores somewhat below average and these people had two completely different ways of dealing with the results. Half of them focused on having below average intelligence. They focused so much on being less intelligent than the others that they scored even worse the second time around when given the opportunity to retake the test.

The other half limited their thoughts to only thinking that they were below average on this particular test. They did not arrive at any kind of conclusions about themselves as people. They did not consider themselves being less intelligent just because they had failed on a single test. When they were given the opportunity to retake the test, they instead chose to focus on performing better this time around, which they also did.

When we focus on what we *are* instead of what we *do*, we hold ourselves back. If we can teach ourselves to focus 100% on what we *do* and stop thinking about what we *are*, then we will automatically become more present. If you can put yourself as a person on the sidelines, then you will notice that you will get better at being present in all kinds of contexts.

Taking daily micro breaks

Each day, try to stop for a few minutes. Let the present moment catch up to you and try to really experience this particular moment in time. When you are present in the moment, it is possible for you to find the truth in your life. Stopping during your day makes it possible for you to really feel what you experience in your mind, your soul and in your body.

Almost everyone wants the most out of life, but when we are only 70% present, we only get 70% out of this particular moment. When you are completely present, you release a free flow of living energy. Your absolute presence makes it possible for you to focus all of your power on this very moment. Consider what you need to become even more present in your life. Is there something in the way you act that disturbs your sense of presence? The last time you felt completely present, what led to this feeling?

The next time you are having coffee with a friend, try putting yourself and all of your thoughts on the sidelines and try to only be present in the moment when you are having coffee. Stop yourself whenever you deviate just the tiniest bit from your zone of complete presence. A lot of people get more present when they experience some kind of crisis. This could be something like a family crisis or something at work. Under ordinary circumstances, people are experts at keeping a number of processes going in the brain simultaneously. What happens during a crisis, however, is that unnecessary processes are shut down as the crisis at hand requires all of our attention. This is also why so many work better under pressure. Last-minute-people need to have a gun to their head in order to focus completely on the task at hand and therefore complete it.

We can learn to identify which processes are unnecessary for the moment and we can also learn how to shut them off, and instead focus on what is important at this particular time. When we wake up in the morning, we are often able to see things more clearly. This is because we have just woken up, meaning that we have as of yet not had the time to initiate a lot of processes in the brain. Just as we initiate processes, we also need to learn how to shut them off. For some, exercise is an effective method for doing this. Others take a nap or meditate (see chapter 20).

When I was 18 years old, I happened to run across an old lady called Asta. She was 100 years old and she was marvelous. At that time, I was working in a retirement home and one afternoon we found ourselves having a cup of tea in her room. Out of the blue, she told me that she thought that I was way too conscious of all of my life choices. She told me that I evaluated all of my decisions too much.

As I did not understand the point she was trying to make, I asked her to explain what she meant. She then told me that for the last 60 years, she had lived her life in such a way that during 90% of her waking hours, she was extremely aware of all of her choices and actions. During this time, she carefully weighed the pros and cons of each everyday decision and she was very careful before stating her own opinion.

The rest of the time (the remaining 10%), she allowed herself to be more unaware. Instead of being guided by her thoughts, she let herself be guided by her gut feeling. She told me that she let go of her conscious self and instead followed an inner feeling. She said that she more or less "forgot" about herself and, to make her point, she said: "I just go where the wind takes me."

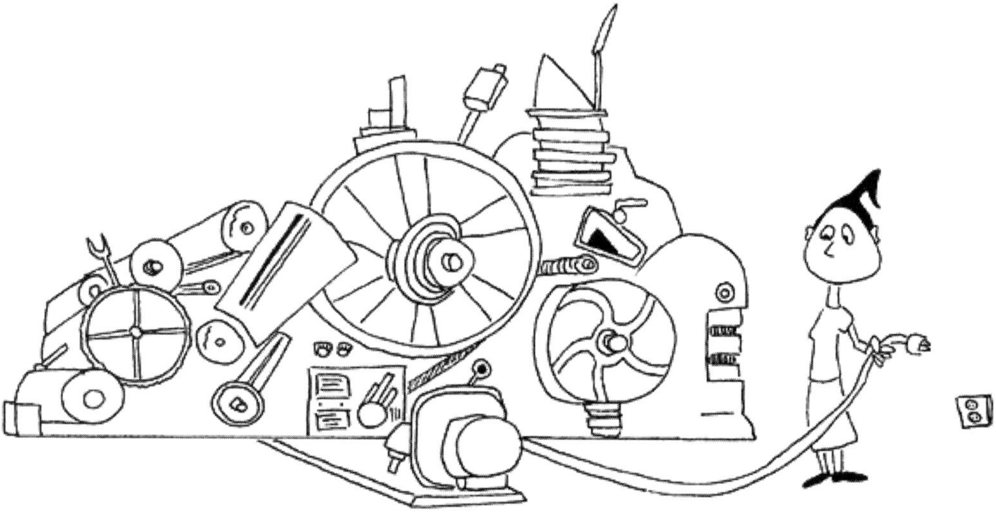

I became intrigued by her notion of letting go of control and instead trusting her gut feeling 100%. I found her to be very brave for, from time to time, choosing to trust her gut feeling instead of her thoughts, because that is what she did. For me, the thought of completely letting go of all kinds of control and forgetting about myself seemed extremely disturbing. When I asked her about this, she laughed and replied:

> My decision to sometimes during the day be more unaware and instead put my faith in my gut feeling is one of the best decisions I have ever made. One thing I regret, however, is that I didn't live like this more often. The times when I have forgotten about myself and only followed my inner feeling have brought me new friends and led me to new adventures. I have left my safe zones and I have had the courage to do more, while also performing better. My self-confidence has improved and I have laughed more. I have automatically become more present, which has made me enjoy life in a completely different way than before. Furthermore, I have also found new ways in life.

She then went silent for a moment. She seemed somewhat thoughtful, while looking straight into my eyes, and then she said: "That is when I have found the right ways in life. But, most of all, I became a free person when I learned to completely forget about myself."

26
Having a winning absence

Did you know that it is possible to temporarily trick fears and uncomfortable feelings by simply being absent?

In the previous chapter, you could read about how we intensify a feeling by being more present. Conversely, we may also reduce a feeling by being absent. It is sometimes necessary for you to be absent in order to be able to deal with certain situations. Just the same way as you may want to enter a feeling and be present, you sometimes also want to leave a feeling and be absent. Most frequently, this has to do with situations where you experience fear or discomfort. If you are afraid of spiders, then you will experience an unpleasant feeling when you see a huge spider in your living room. Being present at a moment like this will make you stay in your feeling of discomfort and, subsequently, you will get even more scared. If, on the other hand, you stop and leave your sense of presence, then you will be able to reduce this fear and feeling of discomfort.

Most people enter and exit different kinds of feelings without even knowing that they are doing so. This happens automatically, but by knowing why it is sometimes a good idea to leave certain feelings, we will be able to deal with discomfort more quickly. Moving away from a feeling may be good when giving a nervous speech, skydiving, getting lost in the woods as the sun goes down or if you are assaulted. Personally, I have learned to do this when I go swimming. It used to be that I every time would feel precisely how cold the water was. I was completely present and every cell in my body could feel this dreadful chill. These days, I always move away from the feeling of being cold as soon as I enter the water, and my experience of going swimming has become much more pleasant.

When you leave a feeling, you get a certain distance to uncomfortable situations. Think about the kind of situations where it would be beneficial for you to create this distance. It could be situations that use up way too much energy or where you get very angry or sad. It could be situations at work, in your everyday life or in your relationship.

Some time ago, a friend of mine told me that she was living with a man she really loved. She thought their relationship was very good, even though her partner had a flaw that made her feel really bad. She told me that her partner had a demanding job and that is why he often sat around thinking about work-related problems when he came home from work. She was mostly very understanding and used to listen to his problems, but there were times when she got sad, as he would sometimes let her bear the brunt of his frustration. This did not happen all that frequently, and she was well aware of the fact that he was trying to deal with this. Nevertheless, this was a big problem for her and therefore also for their relationship.

I explained to her that him being annoyed and frustrated had nothing to do with her, but only with his job. I told her that she should try to create a distance to his behavior by leaving her feelings at these moments. When her partner was back at being his normal self, she could once more enter the feeling in order to be present.

Twelve years ago, I was coaching a number of salespeople. I then had the privilege of coaching a salesperson who was extremely talented at what she did. She had worked as a salesperson for quite some time, but had yet to see her great breakthrough. She had participated in many sales courses and was really struggling to be good at her job. Nonetheless, she was still at a barely average level. I sat for a whole morning listening to her making sales calls, and I have to say that I was very impressed. But at the end of each call something happened – she got nervous. It turned out that the final part of the call got to be too important and exciting for her. The only tweak we had to do for her to finally have her great breakthrough was that she was to leave her feelings at the end of her calls. Just the same way as we can teach ourselves to be present, we can also teach ourselves to be absent at certain times. Here are some methods you may try in order to leave your sense of being present.

Think about something that makes you happy

When you focus your mind on something that makes you happy, you decrease your brain's ability to think about the things that scare you. When you think about something that makes you happy, you create happy feelings and you automatically think less about the things that scare you. Thus, your fears and unpleasant feelings decrease. At the dentist, for instance, or when about to undergo surgery, most people automatically move away from the feeling of possible discomfort. Even when you find yourself in an uncomfortable situation, it is possible for you to move your feelings from fear to joy.

Trick your brain's attention with unpleasantness

When you steer the brain away from that which is uncomfortable, it does not necessarily have to be about things that make you feel good. You may also trick your brain by focusing on completely different things that were unpleasant to you, like that time when you tripped and broke your leg or when you really botched that project at work. You may also focus your attention on situations that were nothing but absurd, like when you happened to drink a glass of milk that was a month old or how sick you got when your friends offered you some surströmming – the Swedish "delicacy" consisting of fermented herring.

When you move your thoughts, you also move your feelings. If you move your uncomfortable feelings from one situation to a completely different one, then it is possible for you to reduce your current fears. In order to illustrate my point by using a simple example, let us imagine that you are stung by a wasp. It is really quite painful and you can feel it hurting. If you were then to all of sudden cut yourself in the finger with a big kitchen knife, then this pain would be so strong that you would, temporarily, forget the pain brought on by the wasp sting. Here, the pain from the wasp sting is replaced by the pain from the knife wound, and this is also how our feelings work. By focusing on prior unpleasant feelings, you may temporarily reduce what you experience as unpleasant.

Laugh and smile

By smiling and laughing, you signal to your brain that you are in a nice and pleasant place. You provide your brain with signals of joy instead of danger. If, for instance, we look at being nervous, then this is a kind of feeling that has been created somewhere and you have certainly done something to create this feeling. When someone asks me how to get rid of his nervous disposition, I always reply: "Find out how you're making yourself nervous, and then do the opposite."

A few years ago, I was asked whether I could help a man to overcome the fact that he always got nervous when addressing large audiences. This was a huge problem for him, as his job required him to frequently deliver presentations.

I started out by asking him what he used to think before giving a presentation. His reply was that he used to think about how embarrassing it would be if he were to make a fool out of himself. He told me that he used to see mental images of himself where his shirt gets damp by him sweating profusely, while, simultaneously, he begins to stutter. One time, he even saw himself passing out for being so nervous. With all of these thoughts spinning around in his head, maybe it is no wonder that he was always so nervous before giving presentations.

Before delivering his next presentation, he instead started to create mental images of him successfully giving the presentation. He also prepared a few jokes he could tell if he started to get nervous. By doing this, it would be natural for him to smile and perhaps even to laugh. A smile or a laugh temporarily tricks your brain away from anxiety and fear to something warmer, funnier and definitely more pleasant. When you let this feeling into your inner self, there is less room for the uncomfortable feelings.

Hum yourself away from the unpleasantness

Have you considered what happens to your current thoughts when you are quietly humming a tune or singing to yourself? Try it! When you start humming a tune, it is no longer possible for the brain to hold on to unwelcome thoughts.

When I was 13, I was deeply impressed by this girl who used to sing in all kinds of settings. We were the same age and she never seemed one bit nervous whenever she was going to perform. One day I asked her how she managed not to get nervous. She then told me that she was always really nervous before each performance, but her trick was to always hum one of her favorite songs when she started to get nervous. This made all of the thoughts making her nervous simply vanish.

Pause your feelings

When we get scared, it is very easy to get swept up by the feeling itself. Consider what happens when you find yourself in a crisis situation. How do you act if someone you like gets hurt, if you end up in a car crash or if you need to take someone in your family to the hospital? Surely, the fear may paralyze us, but we most of the time somehow manage to shut down our feelings to instead focus on the situation at hand. The crisis situation demands all of our attention and, instinctively, we often manage to focus our attention on the crisis itself. What is happening here is that we control our thoughts, and as our thoughts guide our feelings, the difficult feelings are reduced. You will never be able to shut off these feelings for all eternity, but I know that we all have a temporary pause button, which may sometimes be necessary to use. If you practice finding your pause button when you experience fear or discomfort, you will for each time get better at finding it.

Put whatever is unpleasant in perspective

When we experience fear, we often look at it from a dark perspective. Ghosts usually only make themselves known in darkness and, likewise, it is more or less only possible for mental figments to appear during our dark moods. In the morning light, the ghosts disappear, and when our mood gets lighter, the mental figments will also vanish. Adopting a brighter perspective when looking at the fear will make it much harder for it to survive. Let us imagine that you are to give a toast at your brother's 50th birthday party. You experience absolute terror as you know a lot of the people who are going to be there. You are afraid that you will slip up and make a fool out of yourself, and you have an uncomfortable feeling that you will be at the center of attention for all these people. You are now right in the middle of a feeling where you are nervous and uncomfortable. Now move your thoughts to considering how glad your brother will be when you give him your toast. No matter what you say and no matter what happens, you will be a hero who, despite of your feelings, gave the toast anyway. Consider the nice memory you and your brother will have, regardless of how the toast turns out. Consider the great feeling you will experience once you have given your toast. By taking all of the nice feelings resulting from your toast into consideration, you have adopted a lighter perspective on your fear, which will hopefully scare away parts of it.

Everyone who moves away from certain feelings is doing something. Ordinarily, we are not aware of exactly what, as it most frequently happens automatically, but we are doing something. So, what happened with the woman who got sad when her partner let her bear the brunt of his frustration? She called me a while back and told me that she had learned to create a distance to her feelings. Thanks to this, her partner's behavior was no longer an issue for her.

Doesn't this sound natural and self-evident? The more present you are, the more you feel, and the more absent you are, the less you feel. Finding a balance between these two will help you magnify welcome feelings and reduce unwanted ones.

27
Allocate your life energy properly

Every day we only have a certain amount of energy we can spend. We often experience that we have to devote energy on things we would rather not do. But the question is if we really need to spend energy on the things we find unnecessary or if we can learn to save energy for the things that truly matter to us?

Imagine being so fortunate that we had access to unlimited energy every day. Then we would spread energy all over those around us on a daily basis. Unfortunately, however, we all only have a set amount of energy to spend each day. Some days we have more energy, and some days less. Have you considered how you prioritize spending your energy during a day? Regrettably, it is far too easy to forget that sometime during the day, your energy will run out. When do you want your energy to run out? My guess is that you would prefer it to run out when you are about to go to bed or when you are chilling out in front of the TV. If our energy is to last all day, we need to learn how to be economical with it. If we become aware of how we spend it, then we can also learn how to save it.

Some women I talk to may say things like: "My husband is always so grouchy when he gets home from work." But at work, this man may be in a terrific mood. He jokes around, laughs and is pleasant to be around for his colleagues. On the way home from work, he bumps into an old friend from school he has not seen for years, who says: "What's up?! Great to see you!" He gives his old friend a hug and his energy is positively flowing. Later, when he comes home to his wife, his eyes are tired and with a soft voice he says hello and parks himself in front of the TV.

This man means no harm, obviously, but he has spent so much energy throughout his day that he is all worn out by the time he comes home to his wife. During the journey of his life, this man seems to have forgotten that the most important person in his life right now is his wife. From a logical perspective, she really should receive the most of his energy, but this does not happen, as this man has subconsciously chosen to prioritize his job, his colleagues and, in this case, the old friend he has not seen for 20 years.

Women, on the other hand, are much better at saving up energy for the family and their life partner. They usually prioritize their family and their love life, but for many men work and career is number one on their list of priorities. A lot of men strongly identify with their work, and even though they feel that their family is the most important thing in life, they nevertheless devote most of their energy and attention towards work.

First we need to understand what in life we want to spend the most energy on, and then we need to learn how to save energy for these particular things. Let us imagine that you are going on a trek in the desert and that you are only bringing two pints of water. In that case, you are probably very careful how you use your water. You know that you need to save a substantial part of the water for the hottest time of the day, which is between 11 a.m. and 2 p.m. Later, in the afternoon, when you approach your target, you know that you do not need to drink as much as the temperature will be cooler. Just the same way as you economize your water during your desert trek, you also need to economize your energy.

As we only have a limited amount of energy, you may think that you only have two pints of energy for a normal day. On the days when you feel particularly energized, you have three pints, while on the days when you feel worn out you only have a single pint. Regardless of how much energy you have to spend, you know that you have to prioritize how you spend it. In this way, you become aware of the fact

that you need to save energy for the things that really matter in your life. During a normal day, you are faced with a lot of different situations. When you become aware of how you spend your energy, you will realize that there are quite a few situations where you can choose to save energy and thus store it for the more important things in your day. We need to learn to take care of our energy and to become even more aware of how we use it.

There are a number of behavioral patterns that completely devour our energy. Some people devote a massive amount of energy on unnecessary thoughts, whereas others devote half of their daily allotment on being liked. When this person comes home to those who really love her, chances are that she is so tired that she will have a hard time enjoying their love and their company. Maybe you have ended up having a circle of friends who use up a lot of your energy. Then talk to them. A lot of people are not aware of the fact that they use up a lot of energy from those around them and sometimes they just need to be reminded of their behavior. If you politely tell this person what you want out of your relationship, then it will probably become stronger. If the person instead gets upset, then it is probably because your friendship is simply not strong enough.

Going through life, it is easy for us to create various kinds of habits and patterns. These habits later become a part of us and there is a risk that we do not even notice them. Sometimes, unfortunately, we create the wrong kind of habits, which eat up our energy. This could be things like habits at work, how we interact with others or how we deal with criticism. We may have friends simply out of habit who we have actually outgrown and who now only drain us of energy. Maybe, we have behavioral patterns that create problems for us, like overanalyzing things or not trusting people.

Consider whether you are really devoting your energy to the things you feel are important in your life. Ask yourself if it really is worth it – distributing the energy the way you do. Is it worth it that certain things in your life cost energy? If not, consider how you would want to reallocate your energy and, lastly, consider how you are to actually make this change come about. It could be that you are spending way too much energy on people who really are not worth your energy. You may use up too much energy on pointless thoughts or on something you do at work.

Sometime during your day, your energy level will plummet, but just as you lose energy, you may also get more. Like you already know, you get more energy from sleeping well, eating right and exercising. But what else may give you more energy?

Let us return to our example about the desert trek. Maybe you decided to only bring the small water bottle so that your backpack would not be so heavy. Meanwhile, you knew that it would be possible for you to fill up your bottle during your trek. As you knew that you needed to drink a lot of water, you paid extra close attention so you would not miss the watering stations. The question, though, is if you are just as attentive when it comes to life's refueling stations for energy.

People we like are often a source of good energy, and people we do not like are often a source of negative energy. Doing things we like gives us positive energy, and doing things we do not like gives us negative energy. So far so good. The hard part is undertaking a change, which, in the long run, decreases negative energy while increasing the good kind. There are for most people a number of things they do not like, but, unfortunately, we frequently do nothing about them. A lot of things are actually possible to change and we may also include additional things in life that give us more energy. Relaxing, traveling, musicals, nature walks, lectures, knowledge and love are examples of things that may increase your energy.

If we want to give someone energy, then we know that giving compliments is usually a good tool. The fact is that we also get energy when we compliment ourselves. If you rarely receive positive feedback from those around you, then give it to yourself. Practice really listening and absorbing the compliment and practice enjoying it.

New friends, new situations and personal growth are other things that tend to provide you with energy. We need to be careful, though, as we change throughout life. Even though we may not notice it ourselves, we constantly evolve. That is why we should never stop looking for new experiences and interests. We drop some interests because we grow tired of them. This means that we also need to get new interests and new things that energize us in life.

We have previously discussed how we can motivate ourselves through our thoughts, but our thoughts may also steal our energy. If, for instance, you have a big task ahead of you, you normally save energy by breaking it down into a set of smaller targets. If you are experiencing serious grief, then it is easy to only see one great big mountain of grief. If you instead choose to see this mountain as a large pile of smaller stones, then you can focus on simply removing one stone at a time. In this way, it also becomes easier to take one day at a time. If you are right in the middle of building a house, then some days may simply feel hopeless. The feeling of this enormous project that never gets done grows stronger and stronger. We are attaching nails to a board. Meanwhile we see the rest of the hundreds of thousands of nails we have to nail to boards. We will feel much more energized if we can focus on one small part of the project at a time: one nail at a time, one board at a time, one wall at a time, and so on. The mere thought that we are to accomplish an extremely hard challenge may sometimes be too much for us to handle. This feeling may in turn eat up our energy.

Most of us store energy when we do something we like. The energy we store can then be spent on the things that really matter to us. On the days when you have the most energy, stop and ask yourself: "How did I create all of this energy and how may I do so more frequently?"

28
Create an inspiring everyday life

You can achieve wonders if you fill your soul with inspiration. Likewise, your soul may be extinguished if there is no inspiration.

Everyone is born with a roaring flame – an inner fire if you will. This inner fire manifests itself through joy, energy, being curious, a thirst for knowledge and having a zest for life. The inner fire gives us inspiration and makes us come alive, but, frequently, this roaring flame diminishes over time and even gets extinguished for some people. There are those who simply lose the basis for their happiness and joy. But then there are those who let their flames keep on burning throughout their lives. They have learned how to constantly maintain and keep this powerful fire. They have learned to stimulate their inner selves so that they regularly replenish their energy and joy. While some people are nothing but passengers in their own lives, there are those who have put themselves completely at the helm. They have named themselves captains of their lives.

You are the great creator of your own life and it is possible for you to build precisely the kind of life you are dreaming of. But, you need inner strength to succeed and you build this through inspiration. One of the most common causes behind depression is that life consists of way too many musts and all too few sources of inspiration. Give your body the wrong kind of nourishments and your health will eventually suffer. Give your soul the wrong nourishments and your soul will also suffer. Stop eating and you will eventually die. Stop giving your soul nourishment and your soul will also eventually die. We are all different and every soul has its own needs, but one thing all souls have in common is that they need inspiration.

Have you ever felt tired for no apparent reason? Have you considered that your sense of fatigue may just be an illusion originating from the fact that you are bored at that particular time? This sense of fatigue could be a message telling you that you need to fill your life with something more or something else. The next time you feel tired for no reason, try calling a friend or doing something else you enjoy. Also notice how you react when someone is telling you something you have no interest in whatsoever. Some people react by starting to yawn. If this person, on the other hand, is telling us something interesting, then we seldom yawn.

The reason why the sense of inspiration is so tremendously important is because it creates an inner drive. When you feel inspired, everything goes much smoother. It is easier to notice both solutions and possibilities. Inspiration is a flow of energy working its way through the body. Inspiration, most of the time, gives you a better flow in everything you do. When you are experiencing this kind of flow, you perform better, you have more fun and you create a sense of things being easy. If you are inspired, you get happy. And when you are happy, your happiness will automatically rub off on those around you. Before you read on, consider what inspires you and whether you find yourself in these situations frequently enough.

We all know that life may take different turns and that our life may end tomorrow if we are unfortunate. But if you are lucky you could go on to become 90 years old. As we have learned that it is good for us to think positive, let us imagine that you will become 90. Think about how you would like to use this time.

If we count the number of hours we spend on different kinds of activities throughout our lives and then convert these hours into years, then the average person's distribution would look something like this: sleeping for 30 years, working for 15, getting educated for 6 and travelling to and from work/school for 2 years. We also devote 5 years of our lives to everyday tasks like cooking, cleaning, mowing the lawn, etc. What this means is that most of our lives is taken up by the things we see as absolutely necessary. What this also means is that 32 years remain, which we can choose to spend on doing the things we truly enjoy. Remember that we assume that you go on to become 90. If you were to only live until you are 80, then you have significantly less time.

A lot of people wait for others to create opportunities for them, but this hardly ever happens. The fact is that you create your own opportunities. Waiting for someone else to hand you a meaningful and inspiring life could lead to you spending your whole life waiting. Instead of waiting for something to happen, you can start to initiate the changes you need to make in order to be filled with inspiration.

An effective way of getting a good overall picture of how you want your life to look is to write a letter to yourself. Imagine how you want your life to look when it comes to family, work, interests, physical health, mental health, friends, personal growth, economy, leisure time, living arrangements, living standard and so on. Take your time and write as much as possible. To get the absolute best effect, write three different letters. In your first letter, you describe your future one year from now. In your second letter, you describe your future three years from now, and in the last letter, five years from now. Then you put the three letters in three different envelopes with the date marked when you are allowed to open them. When writing a letter to yourself, you get a glimpse of what your life may look like in the future.

In previous chapters, we have discussed how we sometimes switch on our autopilot when life goes into everyday mode. Surely, there are a lot of benefits in switching on your autopilot and hence mechanizing your behavior, but you also need to feel your inner self deep down, where you are truly listening to yourself. This makes it easier for you to take charge of your feelings, which, in turn, makes you more aware of what you need to do to feel good in various situations. The end result is that you never do things just to do them. Instead, you look for meaning in the things you do. If you sometimes have a hard time finding any kind of meaning in what you are doing, then have the courage to stop doing this.

Filling your soul with inspiration from time to time is easy, but it is much harder to create a life structure where you are constantly replenishing your soul with nourishment and hence creating inspiration. The autopilot we have as humans is treacherous. If we find ourselves in a phase of our life we actually do not enjoy, then it may get switched on without us even noticing. Sometimes it is switched on by true survival instinct and sometimes simply out of convenience. People who create a life structure that is constantly giving them nourishment are significantly more aware of when the autopilot is switched on and are therefore able to immediately choose to turn it off. The basis for creating a life structure where you are constantly given nourishment is to consider the kind of contexts you spend your time in.

Is your romantic relationship giving you nourishment?

Unfortunately, there are way too many relationships running on autopilot. Have the courage to stop and ask yourselves what your relationship needs in order to give you inspiration and life force. Ask yourself what you can do to give your relationship more nourishment and what you can do together. It could be small, but important, things like becoming better at listening, doing more things together, surprising each other, showing each other even more love, really showing an interest in each other's lives, taking care of each other, helping each other in achieving your dreams, learning something new by yourself and then teaching this to your partner and so on.

Is your work giving you nourishment?

Your work may be a great source of inspiration. If you have a job that gives you nourishment, then a flow of energy is created, which gives you a sense of inspiration. During your professional life, you spend half of your waking hours at work. Let us say that you, in the best of possible worlds, get eight hours of sleep every night. Your work, including lunch and commuting, takes up about ten hours of your day. What this means is that you only have about six hours left to do the things you really want to do. Unfortunately, you lose another couple of hours to household chores and other so-called musts. So, perhaps you only have two, three or at best four hours left to do the things you truly enjoy. Surely, we should try to do something really good with the remaining hours of the day, but have you considered that it is also possible for you to do something really good with all the hours you spend at work?

If you were given the opportunity to choose whichever profession you could think of, which one would you choose? What would it mean to your life if you had this particular profession? If your current job was to provide you with a source of inspiration and joy, then what would it look like?

Now, I want us to complete a little exercise together. Grab a pen and paper and write down all of the advantages of your current job. Then write down all of the drawbacks. Now look at the list and ask yourself this question: "Do I really want to devote 10 of the day's 16 waking hours to this particular job?" You may come to the conclusion that your current job in fact is your dream job. Or you may arrive at the conclusion that you need a new job or that it is actually possible for you to do something about the negative aspects. A good employer is definitely aware of the fact that the company does better when you feel motivated. Tell your employer what you need in order to be satisfied and motivated at work. If it turns out that the company is unable or unwilling to meet your needs, then you may start to draw up a plan for how to get a new job. I know that it is hard to leave a safe position, but do not stay at a job that does not provide you with the nourishment you need to be at your best with your family, friends and with yourself.

Is your circle of friends giving you nourishment?

This is where the autopilot is particularly efficient. We all change throughout life and it is completely natural that we sometimes evolve in different directions. New friends bring new things to your life and if you are to find room for new friends, you also need to end friendships that no longer correspond with your present life. Consider which topics of conversation are valuable to you and which topics truly inspire you. When meeting your friends, try steering the conversation towards topics that give all of you nourishment. I promise you that one way of giving your friend nourishment is by really listening. By asking questions, you may steer the conversation so that it also gives you nourishment.

Well-functioning social networks and good relationships are emphasized within positive psychology as being tremendously important for people's well-being. An American study shows that our social network prolongs our life. This extensive study also shows that it is just as detrimental for our health to live alone as smoking 15 cigarettes a day or being addicted to alcohol.

Is your leisure time giving you nourishment?

When you are free from all the obligations in life, do you then fill your leisure time with the things you love? When you are doing the things you like, you give your life nourishment. We always have a lot to do and sometimes we forget to give ourselves the nourishment we need to feel inspired. To remind yourself, make a list of all the things you like and treasure in life. Make this list as comprehensive as possible and try to take as many things into consideration as you can. Write down things like laughter, travelling, reading, growth, nature, exercise, music, role models, friends,

"My best friend is the one who brings out the best in me."

Henry Ford

hobbies, good food, candy, new and familiar places, beautiful buildings, animals, caring, knowledge, movies, life, challenges, rest, beautiful colors, children, your parents and siblings, goals, dreams, love, your dog, flowers, picnics, sleeping late, breakfast in bed, the sky or relaxing. Once the list is complete, consider whether you can find more room in your life to enjoy all the things you like.

The autopilot is also switched on when it comes to our interests. Our needs change throughout life, and interests that used to enrich our lives may no longer fill the same needs. Sometimes we need to give up a certain interest in order to develop new and more inspiring ones. When we bring new things to our lives, we grow as individuals and the inspirational power of growing is enormous.

How does media affect you?

What you read and see in the media affects you more than you think. What actually happens to your subconscious mind when you start your day by reading about war and misery?

A few years ago, I was talking to a young boy. He was seven years old and he asked what I like to read. I answered: "In the morning, I read two newspapers." He gave me a curious look and then asked me: "Are these newspapers funny?" I went quiet for a minute and then I replied that I actually did not find them all that funny. I asked him what he liked to read and with a firm and convincing voice he replied: "I only read the kind of stuff I find funny, because that makes me happy. My favorite magazine is Donald Duck." He finished by giving me a good piece of advice: "I think that you should read stuff you find funny instead of those boring newspapers."

This little boy got me thinking and he made me realize that I need to be more careful how I digest the news flow. When we wake up in the morning, our brains have not yet started to initiate all that many processes and thoughts. This means that the space for filling up on information is bigger and, therefore, we are also more impressionable. Instead of starting out my day by filling up on misery by reading about war, poverty and recessions, I now start my days by reading about things that instead fill me with inspiration and joy. I still follow the news flow and read newspapers, but then at times when the effect on my subconscious mind is more limited.

Have you created a home that gives you nourishment?

Last, but not least, we need to create a home that gives us inspiration. Surely the home is an important place for getting energy and power. Create a home that is in harmony with your personality. The closer your home corresponds with your personality, the more it will inspire you. If you like things neat and tidy, then you will probably feel the best by getting energy and power from a well-maintained home. If you like to travel, then maybe you get inspiration from a home that reminds you of past trips or trips you want to make. Fill your home with love – everyone feels good by having love around them. Make your home into a place you really love. Do not get satisfied by only turning your living room into a spot filled with inspiration. Also remember to transform your bedroom, kitchen, desk, porch, bathroom and hallway. Have the courage to change and have the courage to throw out the things that give you negative energy.

If you create a life structure around some of the environments above, then you will automatically fill your life with a lot of inspiration.

At times, we have every chance of feeling truly inspired, but somehow we lose this sense of inspiration. This could happen when problems arise at work or when we meet a friend. This could happen at any time. But, even though we may have lost our sense of inspiration for the moment does not mean that we have to be without it for the rest of the day. It is almost always possible for us to recreate lost inspiration. If you lose your sense of inspiration during the day, try to stop and consider what you can do to get it back. Sometimes all it takes is changing the setting by going to a coffee house, taking a walk or calling a friend. If this does not work, try to recreate your sense of inspiration by planning something nice to look forward to. Or you could look at your list of all the things you like and start giving yourself more time to do these things. Remember that no matter what happens in your life, it is basically always possible for you to recreate lost inspiration.

29
Conquer your fears

People are always striving for different kinds of freedom. Some seek financial freedom, while others want freedom at work. There is, however, a different kind of freedom that is much more valuable – our mental freedom, the freedom of the mind.

Have you considered when you are the most satisfied with yourself? Could it be when you have had the courage to stand up to something that truly frightens you?

Up until a certain phase in our lives, we try to build the life we wish for. We try to create a life that gives us safety and meaning. As the years go by, we get more comfortable and we create more routines in our everyday lives. The need to remain in our comfort zone gets bigger. This sense of safety makes life comfortable, but the question is how much we really grow in the safe space of everyday living. Everyone has certain strengths and we tend to shape our lives around these. We do fine at work. We feel that we have a handle on home and family. We have done what we do in life for years, so we are reasonably good at these things too. We have also learned how to take care of all kinds of routines and everyday chores as best as we can. Life takes place within these safe zones. These safe zones do not put people to the test and there is a risk that they make people blind to their own weaknesses and flaws.

A lot of people turn a blind eye to their weaknesses. Others notice theirs, but do nothing about them. To come to terms with our weaknesses, maybe we need to confront a fear or challenge ourselves. When we notice our weaknesses, we think: "I'll have to deal with that further down the line" or we disregard them and say: "Sure, we all have weaknesses." Sure, everyone has weaknesses. Some we can live with without any problems and some may even be a bit endearing. But we must not

forget that some weaknesses limit us from living life to the fullest. Furthermore, we must not forget that a weakness is a seed for a future flower.

Everyone has their comfort zones and it is very comfortable to exist within these confines. But, if we want to grow, we need to have the courage to step outside these safe borders. We need to face our fears and confront them. Do you remember how good it felt the last time you challenged and conquered a weakness? First you identified it, then you decided to do something about it and then, finally, you did it. When we succeed in doing this, we grow as humans.

It can often be difficult to identify a weakness, however, and we tend to repress the kind of weaknesses that feel like burdens. Sometimes we simply feel that it will take up too much time and energy to work through them and instead we choose to push them aside. At other times, it could be that we are exceedingly aware of the weakness and instead of working through it, we learn to adapt our life to it. In some ways, having weaknesses is a part of being human, but we need to understand exactly which weaknesses limit us.

During life, we end up in situations we would rather not have to deal with. When some people find themselves in situations causing them problems, they tend to think: "Why does this always happen to me? Why do I always get into problems with my neighbors? So, once again I find myself at a job with selfish colleagues. Why am I so unlucky that I always end up meeting the wrong men?" Sometimes we clearly are unlucky and sometimes our problems are caused by others, but they could also be caused by ourselves. It does not necessarily have to be anything wrong with our neighbors or our colleagues – it could rather be that we sometimes create behavioral patterns that lead to these kinds of situations.

A few years ago, I had a job interview with a salesperson who had had seven different employers during the last five years. I asked him why he had quit his previous jobs and he then proceeded to tell me that he had been extremely unlucky as every single supervisor at all of these seven different companies had been bad. His supervisors had simply been rubbish. I found this very interesting, so I asked him about these supervisors. It turned out that he had a hard time specifying anything particular in the way his superiors acted or behaved that would indicate that they were bad at their job. The only thing he could tell me was that they were all very unpleasant. When I asked him why he found these supervisors so unpleasant, he went quiet. He started to fidget and look pale, and after quite some time he said: "Hmm…maybe it's just that I have a hard time having someone being in charge of me."

I never hired this person, but a few years later he called me and told me that he had put a lot of effort into dealing with his problems with authority. He told me that he had had the same job for three years now and that he thought his current supervisor was terrific. It was clear that he had a great weakness, which he had also repressed. He refused to realize that he had an obvious behavioral pattern that had led to problems with his previous supervisors.

The spooky thing about our behavioral patterns is that we are so used to them, and that makes it very hard for us to notice them. It is far too easy to disregard the fact that negative things happening to us could be due to our own behavioral patterns creating these situations. The salesperson with terrible sales figures says: "I have the wrong clients." The warehouse manager who is having problems with his staff says: "Nobody does what I tell them to." The nurse who does not like her job anymore says: "I only have cranky patients." Everyone has different kinds of behavioral patterns and hopefully they are mostly beneficial to us, but there could also be patterns we should try to break. If we make it a habit to sometimes leave our comfort zone, then we will be better able to identify behavioral patterns that limit us. Because when we break our habits, we see our habitual patterns with a different set of eyes. When we notice a weakness, we need to understand what it would mean to us and our life if we were to transform this weakness into a strength. Getting to understand the meaning will give us motivation and power to change.

Do you remember when you learned how to swim? At first, you may have been afraid, but every time you practiced it got easier and easier and your technique improved quickly. Eventually you had practiced enough so that you got pretty good at swimming. Then you ceased to develop as a swimmer and your swimming became more and more routine. Our learning curve looks exactly the same when it comes to driving. If we want to grow as drivers, then we need to go into unknown territory and drive down much trickier roads. We simply need to stop driving out of habit and start to challenge ourselves. We work the same way in life. Sometimes, try thinking differently. Try breaking habitual patterns. Have the courage to defy the power of habit and instead try new paths.

A lot of dreams have been crushed simply because the fear of leaving the comfort zone has been too great. Everyone fulfilling a dream has one thing in common, and that is that they have had the courage to try. The price is a momentary sense of fear and the reward is that the dream will hopefully come true.

Earlier in the book, we discussed how we have preconceived notions about who we are and what we are like. Sometimes we think: "I'm not like that. I'd never dare doing that. That's not me. I could never do that. I could never pull off something like that." Now listen carefully! This is just an illusion. An illusion that does nothing but pigeonholes you and limits your life. As long as you do not harm anyone else, you are free to be exactly whoever you want to be. If you want to be "that way," then that is what you should be. Sometimes we believe that we are afraid of some things and sometimes we say that we do not like this or that, but sometimes it could be because we have actually never tried it. New experiences open up new doors for us. They give us new insights and perspectives.

A few years ago, I had a coaching session with a young woman who was troubled because all of her friends were going to Africa to climb a mountain. Even though she had told them time and again that she did not want to go – these kinds of trips were not her thing – they kept on asking her to come. I asked her: "Why isn't it your thing to go away on adventures and climbing mountains?" Her reply was: "I much prefer going on a simple beach vacation." When I asked her if she had ever taken an adventure trip where she climbed a mountain she said no. "So," I asked her, "how do you know it's not your thing if you've never tried it?" She was starting to look really quite annoyed by now and, after a long moment of silence, she replied: "I don't want to talk about this right now." A few months later, I received a postcard from Africa. She had just climbed her first mountain and wrote that she had found the greatest passion of her life.

We also have to remember that some of the fears we carry with us may be false ones. A friend of mine once had a very unusual fear. He was afraid of salespeople. As I had worked in sales for a number of years, our first meeting got a little awkward. I first met this person at a dinner party at a friend's house. As we were having a glass of wine in the kitchen, he asked me what I did for a living. I proudly announced that I was a salesperson. It took but a few seconds and then he took a couple of steps back. His eyes narrowed, he looked very troubled and he said: "Yikes!" Clearing his voice, he told my friends that he had to go out to get some air as he suddenly felt very sick to his stomach. Then he avoided me for the rest of the night. As soon as I approached, he got noticeably frightened and walked away.

A few years later, I bumped into this person in a grocery store. He approached me, said hello and was very pleasant. He proceeded to tell me that he had undergone years of therapy to find out why he had so many fears. He then told me about the incident that formed his fear of salespeople. When he was three years old, he took a trip to Greece with his mother. One day, while playing on the beach, a person selling souvenirs approached him. This made his mother start running towards him. For some reason, she was somewhat panicked and she was yelling at the top of her lungs: "Stop talking to him! Salespeople are really, really dangerous!" They never discussed this incident ever again. A false fear was created and my friend had to carry this with him for 25 years of his life. Now, we meet a couple of times a year and we always laugh at how afraid he was of me the first time we met.

There are many examples of how our fears may be created at an early age. If the parents are very anxious and constantly remind the child of everything that is dangerous, then there is a risk that their fears may be transferred to the child. A child seeing his mother getting terrified over a spider may end up developing arachnophobia. If the parents are afraid of flying, then this fear may be transferred to the child. If you were unfairly yelled at for stubbornly questioning something as a child, then this may create a fear of conflicts in you.

Quite recently, I was passing by a three-year-old girl who, in an eager and curious way, was about to pet a dog. At the same time, her dad approached her, grabbed her by the arm and said: "Watch out. It may bite you." The girl got terrified and quickly left. Maybe a life-long fear of dogs was created at this very moment.

A lot of people adapt their lives and their behavior to their fears and this often makes it hard to notice them. Living in our comfort zones, we have learned to sneak past the fears instead of confronting them. We need to put in a lot of time and effort into trying to identify our false fears. If, for instance, we find conflicts uncomfortable, we may easily adapt our behavior to avoid these. Unfortunately, we most likely end up avoiding conflicts we actually should get involved in. When we leave the safe confines of life, we will automatically bump into certain fears and we will also have the opportunity to once more evaluate our basic assumptions.

Some of our fears are of minor importance, whereas others hold us back and create mental obstacles. They prevent us from doing the things we really want to do and from feeling really good. If you are afraid of flying, then this fear may prevent you from something as wonderful as exploring the world. Understanding the origin of the fear will make it easier for you to deal with it once it materializes. It will also become clearer to you if this is a false fear or if it was created later in life. Find out the origin of your fears and how they manifest themselves. Consider how these fears create problems for you. It could be that you have plenty of things that bother you about your boss, but your fear of conflicts makes you steer away from bringing this up, which in turn makes you dislike your job even more.

Once you are aware of the underlying causes behind your fears, then you need to consider how you are to deal with them the next time they manifest themselves. Are there any tools or helpful thoughts that can give you strength to deal with the situation? For example, what is the absolute worst that can happen in this situation, how likely is this and what are the consequences? Let us imagine that you finally work up your courage to confront the boss who has been annoying you for so long. The worst that can happen is that you get fired, and the risk of that happening is probably miniscule.

One good method for dealing with uncomfortable situations is to think about something that makes you happy. Thus you trick your own feelings into being happy instead of being afraid (see chapter 26).

If you really want to work through a fear, then there is really only one way. Have the courage to expose yourself to the fear as frequently as possible. I promise you

"The more you expect discomfort, the more you will experience fear."

Abraham Maslow

that you will notice that it is not nearly as dangerous as you once believed it to be. We often tend to magnify whatever we are afraid of, but once we are exposed to it, we find that it was not as terrible as we initially imagined it to be. Before facing a challenge like this, imagine the feeling of how good it will feel after you have had the courage to face your fear. Remember that it will get easier each time. You will time and again be convinced that it was not hard having to face your fear. When we leave the safe zones of life, we face challenges. When we face challenges, we need to make more of an effort and when we make more of an effort, we grow as individuals. And this is when new opportunities arise.

A couple of years ago, I was talking to a little girl who was really sad. She looked at me with her troubled little eyes and asked me: "Why do kids stop playing and having fun just because they grow up? They love having fun and laughing." I thought about this for a long time, but I failed to come up with a good answer. I have to agree with her that it really is quite odd. Why don't we go on doing the things we love throughout life? Why is that so many stop having fun just because they get older? Children often live their lives with a greater sense of mental freedom and they are much better than adults at having the courage to have amazing dreams. They often follow their dreams and impulses without reflecting on all of their feelings. Somewhere inside of you, the playful, curious, laughing and free child remains. Try to get in touch with the child's extraordinary ability to achieve this wonderful mental freedom.

Some people are in prison, while others are imprisoned by their own minds. A fear or a limiting weakness can be likened to a lock. Sometimes it is big and sometimes it is small. The best thing about locks, however, is that there is always a key somewhere. You just have to find the right key for the right lock. This may take some time, but if you look long and hard enough, then you will find the key to your lock. If, for example, you are sad for having been diagnosed with a chronic illness, then your key could be to learn to accept this illness. If you feel let down by someone you know, then your key may be to forgive. If you are terrified of flying, then your key is most likely to incrementally face your fear and thus reduce your feelings of discomfort. For each key you find, the more free you will feel. Focus on finding all of your keys in order to free yourself to a world full of possibilities.

Now that this book is drawing to a close, I want to wish you all the best of luck on your journey towards the best life you can possibly have. Remember – You always deserve the absolute best!

Regardless of whether you have one or fifty years left to live, let this upcoming year be a really good year – perhaps even your best year ever.

Acknowledgements

I would like to start out by saying how grateful I am that you have chosen to read this book. I thank all the amazing people who, throughout the years, have enriched me with their knowledge and life experiences.

A warm thank you to everyone who has read this manuscript and provided me with invaluable opinions and tips along the way.

I would also like to express my thanks to Andreas Siesing for his extraordinary illustrations in the book and to Pia Originalbyrå for the wonderful job with the layout. Many thanks also to Rikard Ehnsiö for his terrific work translating this book from Swedish to English.

Furthermore, I would like to send out a big thank you to brain scientist Joakim Strandberg and psychologist Marie Lundell, who have both given me valuable insights and feedback.

Finally, to all of you who inspired me to have the courage to go for it and to share my experiences and knowledge – a big, warm thank you!

Bibliography

Antonovsky, Aaron, *Unraveling the Mystery of Health: How People Manage Stress and Stay Well* (San Francisco: Jossey-Bass, 1987).

Arnetz, Bengt & Rolf Ekman, *Stress [Stress]* (Stockholm: Liber, 2013).

Ashwell, Ken, *The Brain Book: Development, Function, Disorder, Health* (Richmond Hill, ON: Firefly Books, 2012).

Assagioli, Roberto, *Psychosynthesis: A Manual of Principles and Techniques* (New York: Viking Compass, 1971).

Beck, Aaron T., John Rush, Brian Shaw & Gary F. Emery, *Cognitive Therapy of Depression* (New York: Guilford Press, 1987).

Beck, Judith S., *Cognitive Behavior Therapy: Basics and Beyond* (London: Hodder & Stoughton, 2011).

Begley, Sharon, *Train Your Mind, Change Your Brain: How a New Science Reveals Our Extraordinary Potential to Transform Ourselves* (New York: Ballantine Books, 2007).

Ben-Shahar, Tal, *Happier: Learn the Secrets to Daily Joy and Lasting Fulfillment* (New York: McGraw-Hill, 2007).

Billou, Nicky, *Finish Line Thinking: How To Think And Win Like A Champion* (Seattle: CreateSpace Independent Publishing Platform, 2013).

Byrne, Rhonda, *The Secret* (Hillsboro, OR: Atria Books/Beyond Words, 2006).

Chopra, Deepak & Rudolph E. Tanzi, *Super Brain: Unleashing the Explosive Power of Your Mind to Maximize Health, Happiness, and Spiritual Well-Being* (New York: Harmony, 2012).

Covey, Stephen R., *The 7 Habits of Highly Effective People: Powerful Lessons in Personal Change* (New York: Simon & Schuster, 2013).

Coyle, Daniel, *The Talent Code: Greatness Isn't Born. It's Grown. Here's How* (New York: Bantam Books, 2009).

Cozolino, Louis, *The Neuroscience of Psychotherapy: Healing the Social Brain* (New York: W. W. Norton & Company, 2010).

Csikszentmihalyi, Mihaly, *Flow: The Psychology of Optimal Experience* (New York: Harper Perennial, 2008).

Doidge, Norman, *The Brain That Changes Itself: Stories of Personal Triumph from the Frontiers of Brain Science* (London & New York: Penguin Books, 2007).

Dweck, Carol, *Mindset: The New Psychology of Success* (New York: Ballantine Books, 2007).

Ehdin, Sanna, *Din inre framgång [Your Inner Success]* (Stockholm: Forum, 2007).

Fredrickson, Barbara, *Positivity: Top-Notch Research Reveals the 3 to 1 Ratio That Will Change Your Life* (New York: Harmony, 2009).

Frostin, Anna, *Våga förändra ditt liv med KBT [Have the Courage to Change Your Life with Cognitive Behavioral Therapy]* (Stockholm: Prisma, 2009).

Germer, Christopher K., *The Mindful Path to Self-Compassion: Freeing Yourself from Destructive Thoughts and Emotions* (New York: Guilford Press, 2009).

Gospic, Katarina, *Välj rätt! [Choose Right!]* (Stockholm: Brombergs Förlag, 2012).

Gottfries, Carl-Gerhard, *Emotionell kapacitet [Emotional Capacity]* (Sandared: Recito, 2012).

Graham, Linda, *Bouncing Back: Rewiring Your Brain for Maximum Resilience and Well-Being* (San Francisco: New World Library, 2013).

Grossi, Giorgio, *Hantera stress med kognitiv beteendeterapi [Using Cognitive Behavioral Therapy to Cope with Stress]* (Stockholm: Viva, 2008).

Hanson, Rick & Richard Mendius, *Buddha's Brain: The Practical Neuroscience of Happiness, Love, and Wisdom* (Oakland: New Harbinger Publications, 2009).

Hansson, Rick, *Hardwiring Happiness: The New Brain Science of Contentment, Calm, and Confidence* (New York: Harmony, 2013).

Kahneman, Daniel, *Thinking, Fast and Slow* (New York: Farrar, Straus and Giroux, 2013).

Kantor, J. R., *Principles of Psychology* (Akron, OH: University of Akron Press, 2009).

Klingberg, Torkel, *Den översvämmade hjärnan [The Inundated Brain]* (Stockholm: Natur & Kultur, 2007).

Lauridsen, Irma, *Tankens makt [The Power of the Mind]* (Stockholm: ICA Bokförlag, 2009).

Olson, Lars *et al.*, *Hjärnan [The Brain]* (Solna: Karolinska Institutet University Press, 2007).

O'Shea, Michael, *The Brain: A Very Short Introduction* (Oxford: Oxford University Press, 2006).

Ott, Aadu, *Låt hjärnan vá mé ...!: Utmana det etablerade - utforska det okända [Let the Brain Play a Part Too. . .!: Challenge What's Established – Challenge What's Un-known]* (Gothenburg: Tankespinneriet, 2010).

Peale, Norman Vincent, *The Power of Positive Thinking* (New York: Touchstone Books, 2003).

Peterson, Christopher, *A Primer in Positive Psychology* (Oxford: Oxford University Press, 2006).

Ravikant, Kamal, *Love Yourself Like Your Life Depends On It* (Seattle: CreateSpace Independent Publishing Platform, 2012).

Robbins, Anthony, *Awaken the Giant Within: How to Take Immediate Control of Your Mental, Emotional, Physical and Financial Destiny!* (New York: Free Press, 1992).

Salzberg, Sharon, *Real Happiness: The Power of Meditation: A 28-Day Program* (New York: Workman Publishing Company, 2010).

Schwartz, David J., *The Magic of Thinking Big* (Whitby, ON: Fireside, 1987).

Seligman, Martin E. P., *Authentic Happiness: Using the New Positive Psychology to Realize Your Potential for Lasting Fulfillment* (New York: Atria Books, 2004).

Seligman, Martin E. P., *Learned Optimism: How to Change Your Mind and Your Life* (New York: Vintage Books, 2006).

Sharma, Robin, *The Monk Who Sold His Ferrari: A Fable About Fulfilling Your Dreams & Reaching Your Destiny* (New York: HarperSanFrancisco, 1999).

Simon, Seymour, *The Brain: All about Our Nervous System and More!* (New York: HarperCollins, 2006).

Simonsson, Nisse, *Hjärnpiller [Brain Pills]* (Östersund: Jengel Förlag, 2007).

Simonsson, Nisse, *Hjärnvägar [Paths in the Brain]* (Östersund: Jengel Förlag, 2008).

Simonsson, Nisse, *Varför mår vi så dåligt när vi har det så bra? [Why Do We Feel So Bad When Everything Is So Good?]* (Stockholm: Brombergs Förlag, 2009).

Theorell, Töres, *Noter om musik och hälsa [Notes on Music and Health]* (Solna: Karolinska Institutet University Press, 2009).

Tomkins, Silvan S., *Affect Imagery Consciousness* (New York, Springer Publishing, 2008).

von Matérn, Mikael, *Så blev jag en stjärnsäljare – 44 avgörande faktorer [How I Became a Top Seller – 44 Key Factors]* (Stockholm: Books On Demand, 2010).

Wadström, Olle, *Sluta älta och grubbla [Stop Dwelling and Stop Brooding]* (Linköping: Psykologinsats, 2007).

Wallin, David J., *Attachment in Psychotherapy* (New York: Guilford Press, 2007).

Ware, Bronnie, *The Top Five Regrets of the Dying: A Life Transformed by the Dearly Departing* (London: Hay House, 2012).

Notes